Painted Illusions

Create Stunning Trompe L´Oeil Effects with Stencils

Painted Illusions

Create Stunning Trompe L'Oeil Effects with Stencils

Melanie Royals

NORTH LIGHT BOOKS

CINCINNATI, OHIO

www.artistsnetwork.com

S

Q
698.14
ROY

Library of Congress Cataloging-in-Publication Data

Royals, Melanie

Painted illusions : create stunning trompe l'oeil effects with stencils / Melanie Royals.

p. cm.

Includes index.

ISBN 1-58180-548-9 (pbk.)

1. Stencil work. 2. Trompe l'oeil painting. 3. Mural painting and decoration. I. Title.

TT270.R6797 2004

751.7'3–dc22

2004043368

EDITORS: Christina D. Read and Maureen Mahany Berger
DESIGNER: Marissa Bowers
LAYOUT ARTIST: Kathy Gardner
PRODUCTION COORDINATOR: Kristen Heller
PHOTOGRAPHY: Carol Peerce

METRIC CONVERSION CHART

TO CONVERT	TO	MULTIPLY BY
Inches	Centimeters	2.54
Centimeters	Inches	0.4
Feet	Centimeters	30.5
Centimeters	Feet	0.03
Yards	Meters	0.9
Meters	Yards	1.1
Sq. Inches	Sq. Centimeters	6.45
Sq. Centimeters	Sq. Inches	0.16
Sq. Feet	Sq. Meters	0.09
Sq. Meters	Sq. Feet	10.8
Sq. Yards	Sq. Meters	0.8
Sq. Meters	Sq. Yards	1.2
Pounds	Kilograms	0.45
Kilograms	Pounds	2.2
Ounces	Grams	28.3
Grams	Ounces	0.035

ABOUT THE AUTHOR

A self-taught decorative artist and entrepreneur, Melanie Royals has developed a reputation as a leading innovator and educator in the art of stenciling and decorative painting.

As the founder and creative force behind Royal Design Studio, Melanie shares her passion for paint and its exciting possibilities through television appearances, books, instructional videos, a website and workshops offered throughout the country.

DEDICATION *For my Love, Eric.*

ACKNOWLEDGMENTS

The apparent achievements of one person are facilitated and realized by the activities, encouragement and hands of many supportive people. I would like to thank:

Colleen Sachs for an over-the-top effort to keep up with my continually changing mind and plans to assist with much of the preparation and painting for the projects you find in this book.

Carol Peerce for her artistic eye and awesome photo-framing skills, as well as her ability to get the best shot despite my constant input.

Nita Dyslin, first for helping Carol and then for stepping up to the plate to shoot seemingly endless step-by-step photography with me.

The wonderfully supportive staff at Royal Design Studio: *Tina, Adriana, Lorena, Adelita and Jean*. Thank you for taking care of me and the business!

My great North Light editors: *Maureen Berger* and *Chris Read*. Thanks for all of your support and encouragement throughout the long, creative process.

A special thanks to all of my friends, associates and even customers in the decorative painting industry who have validated my creative efforts with your wonderful comments, feedback and appreciation for what I attempt to provide. It is so blessed and exciting to be able to work in this field, do what I love and be continually inspired by you to do it more. Thank you all!

CONTENTS

Introduction

THE DESIRE TO PAINT AND DECORATE one's own environment spans many centuries, cultures and lifestyles from the prehistoric caves of Pech Merle, France to the tomb of Egyptian God Nebuchadnezzar, from the walls of Pompeii to the palace at Versailles, and down through the ages to our present day. Whether you live in an urban brownstone or a suburban tract house, you have a desire to create a personal living space and a need to make it "your home." Painted Illusions seeks to encourage that desire and satisfy that need.

Decorating a home should be fun, personal and rewarding. One of the best ways to make your home more personal is to put your own creative "stamp" on it and in it through decorative painting projects. There is no shortage of painting information and inspiration in today's world. Television programs, magazines, websites and books on the topic abound. What I provide in this book are some new ideas and new interpretations of old ideas. Not only are these great ideas, they are techniques and projects that are doable. You do not necessarily need any artistic abilities to use these artistic techniques—only a desire to learn them and the inspiration and time to apply them. What makes this book, and the painted illusions it contains, different is the use of a "secret weapon"—the versatile stencil.

Stencils provide such an advantage for decorative art projects and particularly for budding artists. They are easy to use and there are thousands of designs to choose from. Once you learn the basic principles and skills there is literally no limit to the number of ways that you can apply design, pattern, paint and texture throughout your home.

Painted Illusions is designed to provide insight, instruction and inspiration. You can take these projects and ideas as potential "food for thought." Everything offered here is subject to reinterpretation. Take a technique and make it your own by changing the colors, the scale, the pattern or the surface. The creative process is evolutionary and never ending. One great idea leads to another and another...embrace and enjoy!

Mediums & Materials

THE STYLISH STENCILING TECHNIQUES FEATURED in this book don't really require exotic or expensive tools. Most of the supplies that you will need are inexpensive and readily available at your local craft and hardware stores. Additionally, specialty tools, paint, glaze and plaster products can be purchased through the resources that are included at the end of this book.

STENCIL BRUSHES

A range of the most commonly used stencil brush sizes includes brushes sized from ⅜-inch (10mm) to 1-inch (25mm). You will want to have brushes in a variety of sizes on hand for your project.. You will generally use a different brush for each color in your project and for filling in and shading areas of varying sizes. Allow them to dry completely after cleaning before using again.

STENCIL BRUSHES

These round, flat-tipped brushes are designed exclusively for stenciling. You'll need an assortment of sizes for your projects. Larger brushes are used to fill in areas quickly while smaller brushes are used for details.

EXTENDER

Acrylic paints straight out of the bottle are very "heavy." They dry out quickly and build up a film rapidly on the stencil and brush. Unless a heavy, opaque layer of paint is required, thin them with the addition of FolkArt Extender for most stenciling applications.

Extender should be added to acrylic paints in small quantities to create a more fluid, transparent medium for dry-brush stenciling.

Extender changes the viscosity of acrylic paint, making it perfect for creating soft, shaded and translucent effects. The extender will also ensure that the paint will not dry out quickly in its container and will prevent it from building up on your stencils and brushes. Clean-up will be easier too!

ACRYLIC PAINTS

Craft acrylic paints are the most common type of paint used for stenciling projects. They are available in a broad range of colors and can be used on most surfaces. Acrylic paints are quite versatile. The colors can be easily intermixed to create the perfect shade. With the addition of white, acrylics can be made more opaque or they can be thinned with water or extender to create thin, transparent washes of color.

EXTENDER

Simply stir in a few drops of extender for each teaspoon of paint. The extender, which acts similarly to a glazing medium in latex paint, will create more "open time" with the paint, keeping it from drying out and building up a residue on stencils and brushes. Because such a thin film of paint is applied for stenciling, however, the paint will still dry almost instantly.

METALLIC PAINTS

Non-tarnishing metallic acrylic and latex paints come in an extensive color selection and can be used to create stenciled effects that range from understated elegance to outright drama. Metallic paints vary widely in their opacity. Depending on the desired look, they can be used straight from the bottle for stenciling or thinned with extender and glaze mediums for more translucency.

GLAZES

Stenciling with colored glazes is the easy and ideal way to create a very translucent look in your stenciled patterns. Using a glazing medium, tinted with color or added to latex paint, follows the same basic premise as adding Extender to acrylic paints to thin them and increase their translucency. In this case, however, the extender is a glazing medium and a lot more of it is used. Use colored glazes with allover patterns and large brushes, such as a stipple brush, to stencil a lot of square footage quickly and easily. There are two distinctly different types of glazing mediums that can be used.

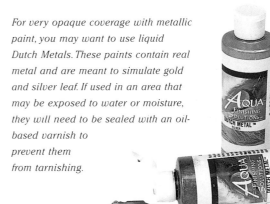

METALLIC PAINTS

These rich, opulent colors are used for the Crewel Embroidery project on page 52. Metallic paints vary from brand to brand and from translucent to opaque. Most manufacturers will tell you the opacity level on the label. Always test metallic paints on a sample before beginning your project.

For very opaque coverage with metallic paint, you may want to use liquid Dutch Metals. These paints contain real metal and are meant to simulate gold and silver leaf. If used in an area that may be exposed to water or moisture, they will need to be sealed with an oil-based varnish to prevent them from tarnishing.

GLAZES

Translucent glazes, sometimes referred to as "scumble" glazes, are meant to be tinted with acrylic colorants or universal tints, not latex paint. These translucent glazes produce an even sheerer look than latex glazes, as they do not have the addition of the white base that all latex paints are mixed from. They can be used for toning and antiquing layers as well as wall and furniture finishes.

Latex glazing mediums or latex extenders must be used in combination with latex paint, generally at a ratio of 4 parts glaze to 1 part paint. Simply mix with the latex paint color of your choice. In addition to a stenciling medium, this type of glaze is most often used for creating easy background wall finishes (faux finishes) over a sealed wall surface. Most glaze manufacturers recommend glazing over a satin or semi-gloss finish latex basecoat. The paint/glaze combination is pictured prior to mixing.

Essential Tools
for Any Project

PAPER TOWELS

Since the key to successful stenciling is off-loading most of the paint from the brush before stenciling, it is imperative to use high-quality, absorbent paper towels, such as Viva or Bounty. Inferior paper towels will yield inferior stenciling results. Trust me on this! Don't skimp on paper towels. Lay out a layer about 3 deep and use them religiously.

TAPE

Decorative painters use a lot of tape. Besides holding stencils in place, tape is used to mask off and protect those areas that we don't wish paints or glazes to be applied to. Also, prior to applying glazed and painted wall treatments, you will want to carefully mask off ceilings, moldings, baseboards and built-in cabinetry. Good quality painter's tape is highly recommended for all these purposes. There are even special tapes for delicate surfaces, such as fresh paint and wallpaper.

ROLLERS AND TRAYS

There are times when a paint project calls for a quick, solid application of color. This is true for base painting as well as certain stenciling projects. It is wise to have an assortment of different sizes and types of rollers handy.

SPRAY ADHESIVE

Use spray adhesive whenever a tight bond of the stencil to the surface is required, such as with stencil embossing, stenciling in corners and on curved surfaces or ceilings. Repositionable Stencil Spray Adhesive is suitable for flat, smooth, painted surfaces. For adhering stencils tightly to textured or plastered surfaces, 3M Spray Adhesive (Medium-Duty) is recommended.

TAPE

Here are an assortment of tapes commonly used in decorative painting projects. From left to right: long-mask painter's tapes, Easy Mask paper tape, Kleenedge tape for sensitive surfaces and narrow striping tape which is used to create pinstriping and grout lines for faux tile and blocks.

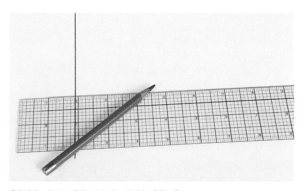

GRID RULER AND PENCILS

This indispensable ruler has markings on clear plastic that allow you to line it up to quickly mark out parallel lines and right angles. Use soft lead pencils or water-soluble watercolor pencils for lightly transferring stencil registration marks and lightly marking lines for stripes, checks, diamonds, etc. Use a light, neutral gray color on light backgrounds and a white or peach color for darker, colored backgrounds. Many times the marks will dissolve when painted over, or they can simply be wiped off later with a damp sponge or paper towel.

BUBBLE LEVEL

Bubble levels are used to establish and mark perfect level (horizontal) and plumb (vertical) lines. The lightweight, plastic models that include measurement markings are the best, and it is helpful to have two sizes. A 12-inch level (shown) is useful for keeping an allover stencil pattern level and plumb as you work. A larger, 48-inch level is perfect for marking out stripes, chair rails and large panels.

Specialty Brushes

BRUSHES

Top: Nylon stipple brush–This colorful brush can be used to stipple and stria, but my favorite use for it is to use it to get glazes onto a textured wall surface and scrub them into the surface. The nylon bristles can easily stand up to rough texture.

Middle: Chip brush–Affectionately referred to as "cheap" brushes, these workhorse brushes are just that. Use them for applying glaze or stain, striaing, pouncing and more.

Bottom: Wallpaper smoothing brush–Find these in the wallpaper department of your local home hardware store. When not wallpapering, you will use it for creating stria finishes in glaze or textural material. It is also the ideal tool for cleaning stencils!

ROLLERS

Left: A ½-inch (12mm) nap roller for painting textured surfaces or rolling on textural materials.

Middle: A textured nylon roller for basecoating rougher surfaces and rolling out glazes on walls and a ¼-inch (6mm) nap pink roller for painting on smooth surfaces.

Right: A dense foam roller for "roller stenciling" and basecoating small areas. (There are also flocked foam rollers for "roller stenciling" and applying smooth finish coats.)

ULTIMATE STIPPLER

I call this brush the "Ultimate Stippler" because it is a specialty brush that can be used with glazed finishes for stippling, stria patterns and softening. My favorite use for it, though, is as a giant stencil brush. I find it particularly wonderful for stenciling out large allover patterns very quickly. Straight acrylic or latex paint will ruin this brush so be sure to use it for stenciling only with paint that has had at least one part glaze medium added to it.

SOFTENING BRUSHES

Top: Hake brush—these brushes are inexpensive China bristle brushes that are ideal for softening latex glazes.

Bottom: Badger brush— a more expensive brush, made from very soft badger hair, traditionally used to soften scumble glazes and for techniques such as faux marble and wood.

ARTIST BRUSHES

Small pointed round brushes are ideal for painting in small details such as highlights and shadows.

Script liners are thin, long bristled brushes that hold a lot of paint. Use them for veins, vines and pin-striping.

Larger round brushes can be used to create soft, cast shadows with thinned paint.

Other Stenciling Products

WOOD STENCILING PRODUCTS

We'll be exploring some illusions that are created on wood in this book. Stenciling on painted wood would involve the same tools and techniques as traditional wall stenciling. However, here we will be working on raw wood. Here are some wood-specific products that will be employed.

GEL STAINS

Water-based gel stains are ideal for staining and stenciling on raw wood. Gel stain has a thicker viscosity than regular wood stain. It is thick and creamy, which makes it the perfect viscosity for stenciling. Water-based gel stains dry quickly, and therefore multiple layers can be applied one after another. Other common wood stenciling tools include chip brushes that can be used for basecoating small projects, cheesecloth for wiping and fine sandpaper for sanding between coats.

GILDING SUPPLIES

Also readily available at art and craft stores are gilding supplies. Inexpensive composition leaf is sold in "books" that contain 25 sheets of thin leaf—plenty for most small projects. Size (the glue that adheres the leaf to the surface) comes in both aerosol and liquid form. A quick-drying spray sealer can be used to seal the leaf and protect it from tarnishing.

WOOD GRAINING TOOLS

Rubber wood graining "rockers" and brushes called "floggers" are ideal for creating an easy faux wood finish and are available at art and craft stores.

SANDING SEALER

This clear medium is applied to wood prior to staining or painting. It seals the pores of the wood, making the surface consistent and allowing stain to go on evenly.

Stencil Care & Cleaning

OK, this is not the fun part! It is, however, worthy of mention because proper care and cleanup will allow you to use your stencils and brushes over and over. Properly cleaned brushes and stencils will also help you to achieve the best possible results with your projects.

To clean your stencils, remove all tape and, preferably, clean the stencil in a place where it will lie flat, such as a kitchen sink, laundry sink or even a bathtub. Clean both sides of the stencil, as some paint or glaze will invariably seep under the stencil. In instances of high paint buildup, spray the stencil with Simple Green before cleaning. If the stencil has a lot of dried, built-up paint, you can soak the stencil in a bath of Simple Green for a day or two and the paint film will almost slide off.

Use a sponge with a slightly abrasive pad or a medium-grit foam sanding block and carefully scrub away excess paint. Take care to avoid scrubbing the stencil too hard, which may cause pointed areas to become bent or delicate bridges to tear.

There may be times, though rare, when it would be more advisable not to clean your stencils. Intricate, delicate, single-overlay allover patterns can be difficult to clean easily. If you have stenciled the pattern with a very thin amount of paint or glaze it may be best to just wipe the stencil carefully with a damp cloth and not scrub it thoroughly.

Another ideal tool for stencil cleaning is a wallpaper smoothing brush. This works particularly well when cleaning larger stencils. You can lay the stencil out on heavy plastic and spray with Simple Green. Brush off the excess paint or glaze and wipe clean with a damp terry towel.

> **✓ TIP**
>
> *Many of the stenciling projects in this book call for the use of stencil spray adhesive. Most of the adhesive will wear off as you are stenciling, but a thin film will remain even after stencil cleaning. If this doesn't bother you (it doesn't bother me!), you can simply store the stencil back in its plastic sleeve. To remove the adhesive completely, you can wipe the stencil down with paint thinner or leave it in a soak of Simple Green for a couple of days and then simply peel off the leftover adhesive.*

Brush Care

Clean stencil brushes immediately upon finishing up your painting. Never allow the paint to dry out in the brush. I have found that mild soaps work best for cleaning. Two popular cleaning agents on the market, Murphy's Oil Soap and Simple Green, both work very well for cleaning brushes. You can put a small amount of cleanser into a container with some water and allow your brushes to soak for a short amount of time. Fill the container just enough to cover the bristles. You don't want to leave the handles and ferrules (metal part that holds the bristles) in water for any length of time as it will cause damage.

When ready to clean thoroughly, use a plastic brush scrubber to remove every trace of paint from the bristles. Continue to clean under lukewarm running water until the water runs clear. Squeeze out excess water with a towel and leave to dry. You cannot use your brushes again until they are completely dry. Remember, stenciling is always done with a dry brush.

Stencil Fundamentals

YOU HAVE PROBABLY ALREADY FLIPPED through this book many times to take in all the beautiful, inspiring photographs showing the painting "magic" that can be achieved with stencils. You're excited, you're inspired, you are ready to paint! Before you grab a brush to begin transforming your home's surfaces into exciting artistic illusions, such as this Tuscan-inspired grape arbor, you'll want to read through this section (you can enjoy these pictures too).

✓ TIP

Adding a Medium—The techniques demonstrated in this section use craft acrylic paints. In order to create a stenciling medium that is more fluid and translucent than regular acrylic paint, FolkArt Extender (or some other sort of glazing or "extending" medium) can be added in small quantities: a few drops per teaspoon of paint.

Successful Dry-Brushing Technique

THE BASIC STENCILING TECHNIQUE THAT IS EMPLOYED throughout this book is what is known as "dry-brush" stenciling. It is also sometimes referred to as "swirling" or "hard-edge" stenciling. All these terms apply because, basically, you are using a dry brush with a swirling motion to create a hard-edged stencil print. The finished look that is achieved is dependent on the type of paint that is used, how much pressure is applied to the brush, and where and how much color is built up. All of these things are under your control. Let's explore how to go about getting "control" of your stenciling.

The dry-brush stenciling technique allows you to apply very thin, sheer layers of paint through the stencil. The result is a layer of translucent color that allows the background or prior layers of paint to shine through, producing an interplay of color and/or texture. This melding of layers and colors creates the illusion that the applied paint is not something foreign but is rather an integral part of the surface to which it is applied.

PAINT

The first key to successful dry-brush stenciling begins with very little—very little paint that is! No matter what stenciling tool, technique or medium you are using for a particular project application, you will be applying it with a very dry brush. This means that after loading your brush with paint (or glaze or stain), you will be removing most of the paint off the brush before stenciling with it. While this may seem like a waste of paint, not to mention physical energy, it is the most important concept to keep in mind when trying to achieve the type of stenciled effects featured in this book.

1 Dip the stencil brush straight into the paint, loading just the tip of the brush evenly with paint.

3

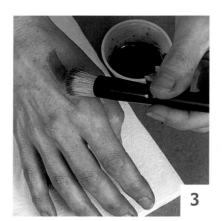

2 Now off-load the brush by rubbing it very firmly on the paper towels in a circular motion. Press hard enough on the brush to create circles of paint that are at least twice the diameter of the brush. This will ensure that the brush is evenly loaded as well.

You can test the brush by rubbing it lightly across your hand. If there is paint on your hand, you have too much paint on the brush. The idea is that the paint should be released from the brush only through a firm pressure. Now go wash your hands!

Dry-Brushing, continued

POSITION

Where you position the brush in relation to the stencil opening is the second key to creating the effects that you want with stencils. Positioning the brush mostly inside the stencil opening will create an even, opaque, graphic look. By moving the position of the brush so that just a small portion of it enters into the open stencil "window," you will develop the "fade-away" effect that creates the look of dimension. This fade-away technique is used to fashion trompe l'oeil illusions of dimensional forms as well as to create high contrast shading within multi-overlay stencil designs.

1

The position of the brush in relation to the stencil edge will affect the finished look.

2

Stenciling with the brush positioned mostly inside the stencil opening (or window) will result in a more solid, even distribution of color.

3

Positioning the stencil brush on the outside edge of the stencil window allows just a small area of the brush to hit the exposed area as you stencil. This creates a completely different look.

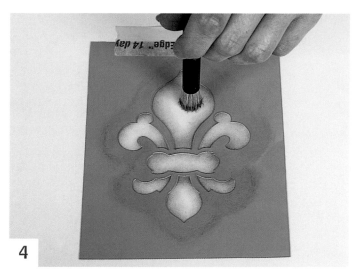

4

The dry-brush stenciling technique uses a swirling motion, as opposed to a stippling or pouncing motion. Move the brush in small, regular circles as you move around the perimeter of the stencil design, building up a nice sharp edge and more depth of color. For a dimensional look, ease up on the pressure on the brush as you move towards the center, to create a lighter value of color.

5

Here, the effect is that of a sharp, crisp, well-defined line of darker color that "fades away" towards the middle of the stencil opening.

PRESSURE

Finally, the third key to ensuring your stenciling success comes with learning to control and manipulate your pressure on the brush effectively. The amount of pressure you place on the brush determines the depth of color in your stenciled print. More pressure on the brush creates deeper, darker color. Less pressure leaves a print with lighter, more transparent color. Some of the projects in this book call for simple, uniformly stenciled prints. In some cases, the stenciled prints will be solid and opaque. In other cases the prints will be soft and translucent. The end result will largely be determined by the translucency of the color and the medium that is used, as well as the pressure placed on the brush.

There are two ways to create more depth of color. The first is to stencil multiple layers of color. The second is to apply more pressure on the brush. The pressure comes through your shoulder. A firm but lighter pressure will leave a light blush of color. A heavier pressure on the brush will leave more paint on the surface and create a deeper value of color. It is a good idea to practice doing value studies such as these on scrap paper. Experiment with differing amounts of paint and pressure on the brush to get a feel for your own "hand." Soon it will all become second nature!

Stippled Texture

An easy way to add texture and additional color to a solid or shaded print is to stipple a lighter or darker color over top of it.

1 Stippling involves a straight up and down, or pouncing, motion with the brush. You can shade and add dimension with this technique as well, simply by concentrating more depth of color in specific areas.

2 Stippling works well for adding darker color as shown or for adding a lighter, highlighting color over a darker background. It is also ideal for adding texture and contrast when stenciling with metallic paints.

Fade-Away Shading

Fade-away shading is used to develop dimensional looks that create a sense of depth and space. Fade-away shading allows you to "sculpt" with paint. You can use this technique to make a flat solid shape appear rounded and dimensional by shading the form. Form shading is shading that occurs on the object itself. You can use shading to define the form by using a soft, gradual shading technique on the areas of the object that recede or move away from the source of light.

This shading technique takes full advantage of the unique qualities stencils provide. First, stencils provide an edge—figuratively and literally! The mylar edge of the stencil controls exactly where the stenciling is applied, protecting the surrounding background from paint or other mediums. The edge of the stencil opening allows you to use the brush in a way that creates a build-up of color along the edge, with a gradual fade-away of color towards the center.

SHADING TO DEFINE SPACE

Fade-away shading is also used extensively with multi-overlay stencils to visually separate the adjoining elements and to define them spatially for the viewer. For instance, you must determine if the object you are painting is in the foreground or the background. Objects in the foreground will receive the most direct light and therefore will receive soft shading simply to represent their form and shape.

Objects that are placed behind other elements in the background will be blocked from the light, and will be naturally darker. Additionally, the foreground elements will cast shadows onto them at the point where the two elements come together.

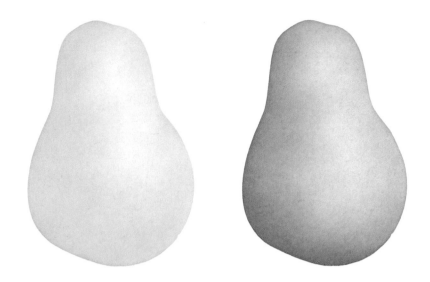

FADE-AWAY SHADING

Here I have concentrated a buildup of color and shading on the lower left side of this pear shape to represent both the fact that it is a rounded, cylindrical object and that the light source is coming from the upper right. The easiest way to represent light on an object with stenciling is to simply apply less color to that area, allowing the lighter background to shine through. In effect, you are preserving the light source in your painting, rather than going back to add it later with a lighter color.

SHADING TO DEFINE SPACE

In order to visually separate the various leaf elements in this design and to define their relationship to each other and to the viewer, I have used fade-away shading to create both shadow and dimension on the leaves as well as to separate the layers. The leaves which are "forward" would receive the greatest light, whereas those that are "behind" them would be blocked from the light. The areas that receive the deepest amount of shading color are the points where the background leaves intersect and go behind the leaves that are in the foreground.

Roller Stenciling

Dry-brush stenciling offers a lot of control and is perfect for creating shaded and detailed looks and illusions with stencils. Roller stenciling doesn't give you quite the same amount of control or connection to your stenciling, but it does have the advantage in certain situations, particularly when a solid, graphic look is desired. Additionally, if the stencil and/or the area to be covered is large, roller stenciling could be ideal.

Roller stenciling works best on smooth or semi-smooth surfaces. It is not recommended for medium to heavily textured surfaces, however, because any extra pressure that you place on the roller to get into those nooks and crannies will also push paint under the stencil in undesirable ways. The best type of roller to use is a 4-inch dense foam roller. For larger projects, place latex paint in a paint tray. For smaller projects, you may want to just use liquid craft acrylic paints which have been laid out on palette paper or a styrofoam tray or plate.

Just as with dry-brush stenciling, roller stenciling should be applied with an off-loaded roller and depth of color should be built up by painting with thin multiple layers. An attempt at one quick, heavy application of paint will only give you a mistake to fix later.

1 Load the roller with paint and distribute it evenly by repeatedly rolling over the textured part of the paint tray or a clean part of your palette. Lining the tray with a plastic sleeve or bag will make cleanup a lot easier.

2 Off-load the excess paint by rolling lightly a few times on a stack of paper towels or absorbent paper. Note: Don't use newspaper, as the ink may come off on your roller.

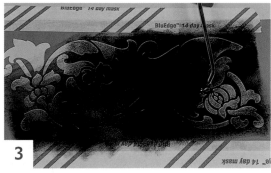

3 Using a light, even pressure, roll over an open area of the stencil repeatedly to cover. It is always better to exercise patience and roll over an area multiple times rather than trying to get the paint on in one heavy application. That will invariably cause the paint to be pushed under the stencil.

4 Lift the stencil to make sure that you don't have excess paint seeping under. Adjust your pressure on the roller accordingly.

5 When finished, remove the plastic bag from the roller tray as you turn it inside out, trapping the leftover paint. Squeeze all the paint into one corner, then cut a small hole in the bag. Now squeeze the excess paint back into the paint can and toss the bag!

Ultimate Stenciling

I call this Ultimate Stenciling because it uses the Ultimate Stippler brush and is the easiest and quickest way to apply an allover pattern to a wall or other large surface area.

1

Place the tinted glaze in an 8-inch (203mm) paint tray. Use a small brush to apply a thin layer of glaze to the textured portion of the tray.

2

Load the brush from here. Because you will want to remove most of the glaze from the brush, you don't want to dip it directly into the wet glaze.

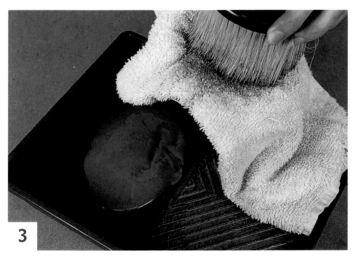

3

Off-load excess glaze onto a terry rag. Note: With the addition of a glaze medium, paint or color becomes "wetter" and will tend to disperse and travel more easily on the surface (that's the whole point of adding the glaze). Therefore, be especially conscientious about off-loading the brush well.

✓ TIP

Spraying the back of the stencil with spray adhesive will help to keep it secured to the surface, but will not keep excess paint from seeping under.

4

On the wall surface, you will stencil with the same dry-brush swirling technique as with a smaller brush. With "Ultimate Stenciling," however, you can expect to stencil out several square feet in a matter of minutes.

Wall Glazing
Tuscan Wall Treatment

THIS SIMPLE WALL TREATMENT, done with latex glazes, provides a rich, warm finish that can transform an otherwise plain wall into a rich backdrop for home furnishings and any number of additional stencil applications. It can be done in many color variations to suite a particular color scheme or design setting. It is done in two layers but you can also choose to do each layer alone for a simpler version.

✐ TAKE NOTE

When considering alternative color options, look to the furnishings and fabrics that are in the room for your color cues. Latex glazes are ideal, particularly for beginning wall glazing projects, because you can simply choose paint colors from a deck and have them mixed. For a foolproof, elegant look, choose colors that are closely related in value and hue. If a deeper finished tone is desired, start with a background color in a light to medium value of the colors that you are mixing with your latex glaze.

PREPARATION

Basecoat walls with two coats of Benjamin Moore Straw. Allow to dry for a minimum of 2 days and up to 2 weeks for a full cure. The better cured the underlying paint finish, the easier and more successful your glaze coats will be.

Mix the 4 separate colors of latex paint with a quality latex glaze at a ratio of 1 part paint to 4 parts glaze. For an average-sized room of approx. 400 sq. ft. (36 sq. meters) you will need about 1½-quarts of the HC-41 glaze mix and about a pint of each of the other colors.

SUPPLIES

Benjamin Moore Latex Paint
(AquaPearl) Basecoat:

Straw (BM 2154-50)

Glaze colors:

Richmond Gold (HC-41)

Valley Forge Brown (HC-74)

Kennebunkport Green
(HC-123)

Georgian Brick (HC-50)

AquaGlaze latex glazing medium

foam brushes or rollers

Ultimate Stippler brush

terry towels

hake brush (for softening)

1

Working in small, irregular areas (approx. 3' × 3') apply the HC-41 glaze mixture to the wall with a 3-inch (76mm) foam brush. Use diagonal, uneven strokes, leaving at least half of the background uncovered.

2

Now take the Ultimate Stippler and use a hard, swirling, circular motion to rub out and move the glaze into the open areas on the wall. The circular motion itself will tend to even out and blend the glaze very effectively, providing that you haven't applied too much paint to the wall.

✓ TIP

The natural tendency with this finish is to apply too much paint. This will make blending out the glaze difficult and time consuming. It may take a bit of practice to get a feel for how much paint to apply. If you run into trouble at the start, simply wipe it away with a damp towel and start over.

If done correctly, this paint treatment will leave just a blush of soft color of varying depth across the wall. This in itself is a wonderfully quick, easy and elegant treatment for walls. It is also the perfect background for stenciled finishes and for ceilings. You may want to stop here. The next steps, however, will add more depth and color, plus the vibrancy that creates a warm, Mediterranean look. As with all wall finishes, the number of layers and the variety of colors used are completely up to your own personal preferences and needs!

Wall Glazing

3

Blend out the edges of the paint "to infinity," meaning that they should just fade out completely without leaving hard edges or lines. When you begin an adjacent area you will apply the paint just beyond where you have left off and work back into the previous area.

Use the Ultimate Stippler as a softening brush, if necessary, to remove any brushstrokes that may be left. Simply brush very lightly across the "top" of the glaze in varying directions.

4

Allow the previous layer of glaze to dry a minimum of 24 hours. Apply the remaining colors of glaze with foam brushes, all at once, to a small workable area. You can vary the amount of each color used to suit your own taste. Over an entire room the color balance will change slightly from area to area as you may use more of one color "here" and less "there."

5

Mix and blend the colors a little with the foam brush. Wet a terry rag and wring out well. Fold it in half and then in half again, creating a small pad.

6

Use the rag in a sliding/skipping motion over the wall, blending the colors together so that you don't see an edge where one color ends and the next begins. Continually turn and change the direction of your hand, as well as your pressure, so that you end up with a random, natural look. As with the first part of this finish, you will want to fade out your edges and then work back into them when you move on to the next area.

You may like the look of the rag blend as it is and can stop here. If you want a softer, more blended look, use an inexpensive hake brush to soften the glaze and "melt" it into the background. The purpose is to eliminate all evidence of the "method of application." Softening the glaze will help to make it look like it is a part of the surface rather that just another layer of paint/glaze. Use very light pressure on the brush—just skimming over the surface—to preserve the essence of the texture that has been created with the rag blend.

7

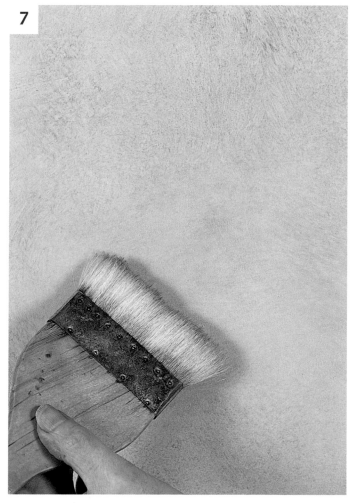

Freeform Stencils
Tuscan Grape Arbor

GRAPES AND IVY REPRESENT an enduring and ever-popular design theme. This richly stenciled, free-form arbor on the Mediterranean-hued Tuscan Wall Treatment creates a warm, relaxed setting in which to dine, work or play.

This project requires some patience and practice time. Stencil out proofs of the different design elements to get a feel for the use of color and shading. You can use these later to help you plan your free-form design.

✓ TIP

Free-form stenciling involves stenciling either individual elements or small groupings of elements in a non-repetitive manner. The result is a design that looks more hand painted than stenciled. The stenciling and design can be easily customized to accommodate different architectural features. For instance, you may just want to use the stenciling around a pretty arch or doorway.

The room shown was fairly plain and ordinary, so an interesting architectural element was created by stenciling a scroll motif as a border to look like a wrought-iron trellis. This border ties the room together while providing an element on which to "grow" the free-form ivy and grape motifs.

SUPPLIES

Royal Design Studio Stencils:

   Palazzo Scroll

   Grape Clusters

   Grape Ivy Vine

Modern Masters Metallic Colors:

   Statuary Bronze

   Copper Penny

FolkArt acrylic colors:

   Bayberry

   Olive Green

   Dapple Gray

   Real Brown

   Raspberry Sherbet

   Purple Passion

   Wicker White

   Terra Cotta

   Teddy Bear Tan

   Burnt Umber

assorted stencil brushes

long script liner artist's brush

small pointed round artist's brush

PREPARATION

This stenciling is done on the background that was created in chapter 1, following the steps for the "Tuscan Wall Treatment." To create the effect of the trellis, the scroll stencil is flipped every other time and is positioned closely together. To make it easier, measure out and mark the placement so that you can stencil out all the scrolls that go one way before cleaning the stencil and flipping it horizontally to stencil the "in betweens".

With free-form stencils such as these, it is very helpful to create stenciled proofs of the finished sections of leaves and grape clusters. You can use these proofs to help "design" your stenciling and guide your placement. The beauty of free-form stenciling is that you can stencil as much or as little as you want, where you want it. The proofs will give you a visual reference and starting point. The proofs can be stenciled on newsprint, tracing paper or ideally, on translucent frosted mylar or acetate.

1 Stencil both overlays of the Palazzo Scrolls solidly with Statuary Bronze. Complete the base coating of the scrolls throughout the entire room.

2 Replace the stencils and stipple over the Bronze with Copper Penny, aiming for about 80% coverage and obvious texture.

3 Now shade just along the edges where the leaf details on the scrolls overlap, to create depth and interest. Use Burnt Umber and a smaller 3⁄8-inch (10mm) brush to shade tightly in these small areas.

4 A detail showing the finished scrolls.

Freeform Stencils

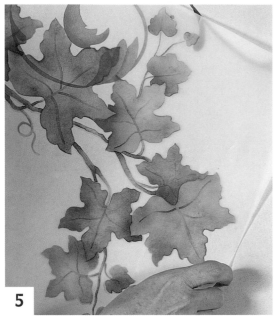

5

If you have created some stenciled proofs of the different design elements, you can use these to determine where you want to paint the various free-form leaf and grape designs. Here, I'm using a section of a stenciled proof for placement.

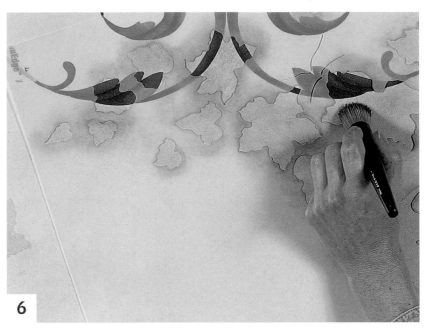

6

Use sections of the Grape Ivy Vine stencil to create some leaves that will fill in space quickly. These will become the "background" leaves. They should be stenciled lightly and evenly with Dapple Gray, using a 1-inch (25mm) brush. Do not shade on this layer—keep it very flat and indistinct. There are veins included with the stencil but do not stencil these on the leaves.

7

With the background leaves in place, it is time to stencil the foreground leaves. These leaves will be well defined, colorful and fully shaded. In order to establish a good base of green color to build on and to cover the background finish, stencil the main elements first in Bayberry. This green has a lot of white in it, is very opaque and will provide better coverage than a more translucent, true green color.

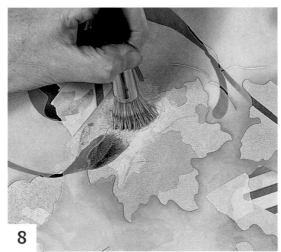

8

For a more realistic look, you can paint some of the leaves, or portions of leaves, to completely cover the scrolls. Add some Wicker White to the Bayberry to make it even lighter and more opaque. Stipple heavily over the previously painted dark scroll in the areas you want to cover. It may take 2–3 layers of paint to cover completely. Allow the paint to dry between layers. Later, in step 19, you'll see how to go back and make some adjustments in order to paint other leaves as if they are fully behind the scrolls.

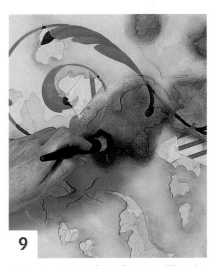

9

Go back and use Olive Green to fill in the leaves with a brighter green color. Because leaves are flat, do not shade them dimensionally (darker around the edges and lighter in the middle.)

10

11

12

For a more natural look, each leaf should receive varying amounts of all of the colors listed, with the green being dominant. The raspberry and purple colors will add more interest and help to visually tie the leaves in with the grapes to come. The Teddy Bear Tan can be used to create the look of dappled sunlight and lighten the leaves to make them come forward. All of the colors should move randomly through the leaves (no sense of pattern). Using a very dry brush will ensure that the colors will be well blended.

The Real Brown is used mainly to create deeper shadows where the leaves overlap, but should be used sparingly in other areas of the leaves. Create more contrast in the areas that call for the deepest shading by pressing harder on the brush and building up more color. I like to add a little bit of darker color down the center of the leaves and along the vein line, to give them a little more dimension.

The grapes will be based in with the Bayberry in the same way as the leaves. The advantage of first lightly basing in the complete design, besides covering the background, is that it gives you a good visual reference for the complete design. You can now easily see how the different elements relate to each other and shade and color them accordingly. Also, the green base works very well to create more realistic-looking grapes and allows them to relate better to the leaves.

✓ **TIP**

With all the leaves colored, you will now need to add the shading and contrast that define where the leaves are in relation to each other and to the viewer. The leaves that are most forward will receive the most amount of light. They will get only light touches of shading with the Real Brown, perhaps down the center or at the base of the leaf. Where there are leaves that overlap, you will add deepest shading at the point where one leaf goes "behind" another one.

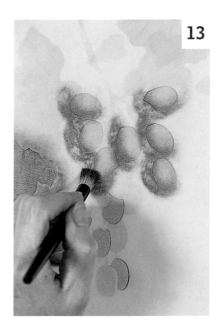

13

The grapes will be colored and shaded mainly with the Raspberry Sherbet. Allowing some of the Bayberry to remain as a "highlight" provides a more natural and unifying look. In this context, the grapes are being shaded as if the light were coming from the upper right. That means that the soft form shading will be deepest on the lower left sides of the grapes and will fade to nothing as it comes around toward the direction of the light source.

Freeform Stencils

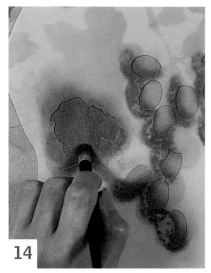

14

The leaves that are included as part of the grape cluster will be colored and shaded in the same way as the other leaves. Here, I am adding some of the Raspberry Sherbet used in the grapes to color the leaves.

15

This detail shows the grape cluster completed. Raspberry Sherbet is used on the grapes for the basic shading and coloring, over the Bayberry Green base.

16

To create even more dimension, add deeper colored areas by using Purple Passion.

17

Use Real Brown to stencil in stems and branches. I am now working on a different set of grapes. You can see that I have elected not to stencil the upper elements of the design, as that top stem does not relate to the leaf behind it. That group of leaves was created earlier and I am "working in" the grapes around them. In free-form stenciling, you can selectively eliminate elements that are unwanted or unneeded simply by not including them. I have not stenciled in the veins. Later, I will paint these to achieve a more natural, hand-painted look.

18

As cylindrical objects, the grapes will be shaded according to the light source in two ways: their relation to other objects and their relation to the light source. The Real Brown is used to shade the grapes that are in the background and are blocked from the light. Shade darkest along the overlapping edges.

19

When all your fruit and leaves are finished, you can go back and re-stencil the scrolls where some of the leaf color has overlapped it (refer back to step 8). Finish up with some hand-painted accents.

✓ **HAND PAINTING TIP**

Adding some simple hand-painted accents to your stenciling can add more realism to your illusions. The idea of hand painting may seem intimidating if you're a novice. But it is a useful skill to have, and easy to learn and accomplish with just a little practice.

20 Use a long script liner to create delicate veins for the leaves. Pull these strokes in the direction of growth—from the base of the leaf out towards the tip. Notice that the stroke ends in a delicate line, just short of the tip of the leaf.

21 After creating all the center veins, pull delicate side veins off the center line and out towards the pointed tips. Notice how these side veins curve and arc away from the center. They do not come out at right angles!

22 A small pointed round brush is perfect for adding highlights or shadows, especially on architectural elements such as these wrought iron scrolls. As a final finishing option, use thinned Terra Cotta to create highlights. Press down on the brush in the middle of the stroke to fatten the line. Pull away from the wall as you finish the stroke to leave a nice, thin tail.

✓ TIP

- *Use fresh, thinned paint. Fluid brushwork requires fluid paint. Don't be tempted to use up that stencil paint you've had sitting out for hours for your liner work. Put out fresh paint and thin it with water or extender. The amount of thinning depends on the type of brushstrokes you will be painting. For painted highlights, thin just slightly. For liner work, such as veins, vines or to paint translucent shadows, you will probably want to thin the paint at least 1:1 with water or extender.*

- *Unlike stenciling, you should always wet an artist's brush before use. Keep a container of water handy for rinsing.*

- *Fully load the brush. If you dab just the tips of the bristles into the paint, you won't get very far. Fill it up! Load the brush by pulling it repeatedly through the thinned paint.*

- *Rinse your brush often. Your paint and brushstrokes will start to become thick and gloppy if you keep going straight back to the paint. Rinse the brush often to preserve nice, clean, uniform strokes. This will help to preserve your brush as well.*

- *Begin and end each brushstroke on the tip of the brush. Start and end each stroke with the brush held perpendicular to the surface to create a fine line. The more you push down and flatten the brush on your stroke, the fatter the line you will create.*

A detail of the Tuscan Grape Arbor.

CHAPTER 3

Stencil Embossing

STENCIL EMBOSSING RAISES THE ART of stenciling to new heights—literally! Stencil embossing involves creating a raised (or dimensional) image or pattern by applying a textural medium to the surface through a stencil. This simple act opens up a world of possibilities, many of which will be explored and exploited in later projects in this book. As if the prospect of quickly and easily creating a sculptural, raised image weren't enough, you can alternately combine this stenciling technique with many other techniques, paints and materials to create illusions such as faux crewel embroidery, embossed velvet, or even embossed leather, tile, plaster or metal.

Materials

For a good embossed stencil print you will need to use a textural material that can easily be applied with a trowel and will hold its shape when the stencil is removed. There are many suitable medium- to heavy-bodied textural materials on the market today. Some are readily available in art, craft or home hardware stores, while others are specialty items such as Venetian Plaster and resin-based stone-like materials that can be ordered through the decorative paint manufacturers listed in the Resource Section at the back of this book.

The easiest, most inexpensive and readily available medium to use is pre-mixed joint compound. It goes on like butter and is easy to clean from tools and stencils. It is ideal to use in areas that will not receive any wear or tear, so it is not suitable for furniture or low wall areas. Its major drawbacks are that it can be easily chipped or damaged and that it is very porous and needs to be well sealed with primer or paint prior to any other decorative treatments that you might want to add.

This elegant cornice was created by stencil embossing a classic Romanesque Frieze just below the ceiling line with premixed joint compound. Real wood molding was then added at the top and bottom. The whole frieze area was primed and painted in an off-white satin latex and then simply antiqued with a Raw Umber glaze.

> ✓ **TIP**
>
> *There are ready-mixed options available that will provide a durable embossed print, such as Golden Hard Molding Paste.*

ROYAL PLASTER

You can easily create a more durable plaster for embossing by following a simple recipe and mixing ingredients from the hardware store. I call this medium "Royal Plaster." This plaster mix can be sanded and will be quite durable when dry. The glue in it will also make the final product less porous than ordinary joint compound, although it will still retain a slight porousness.

"Royal Plaster" does not have a long shelf life, two days at the most in an airtight container, so you should only mix up small batches at a time. It will also become heavier the longer it sits, though you can always add a little water to thin it. When first mixed, it will be more fluid than joint compound, and your embossed images will tend to round slightly at the edges. This can actually create a very nice effect.

ROYAL PLASTER RECIPE

1 *In a plastic container that has an accompanying lid, place 2 parts premixed joint compound*

2 *Mix in 1 part white glue and stir well.*

3 *To thicken, add up to 1 part powdered joint compound, stirring in just a little at a time. Stir until well mixed with all lumps removed. The powdered joint compound comes in different "setting" times. 90-set is the highest and means that, when mixed with water, the compound will set up (begin to harden) in 90 minutes. This is the longest setting time available and is preferable.*

Tools for Embossing

TROWELS AND OTHER TOOLS

Stencil embossing involves using a trowel to apply a layer of material through the stencil opening. There are many different types of trowels to choose from, including metal trowels, but plastic is my preference for most jobs. It is more pliable, inexpensive and easy to clean.

You will use different sizes of trowels depending on the size of your design and project. Plastic taping knives can be found in the drywall section of your home/hardware store and come in a range of sizes.

Small pieces of 30mil styrene are useful for embossing smaller designs. They are flexible, so you can round them with your hand to avoid creating lines in your embossed design.

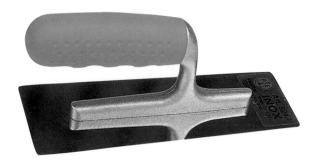

VENETIAN TROWELS

Another type of specialty trowel that is used mainly to apply a plaster background is a Venetian Trowel. This trowel is used in a sweeping motion across the wall. It can also be used with embossing techniques to apply a smooth, even layer of material through a stencil.

STENCIL CHOICES

Multi-overlay stencil designs are not recommended for beginning embossing projects because once you have embossed the first overlay, you no longer have a smooth, flat surface on which to place the second overlay. Successful embossing requires that the stencil be tightly bonded and flush with the surface to prevent the material from being pushed under the stencil as it's applied. That is not to say that you could never emboss a multi-overlay design. It is possible, particularly if you are using a low-relief application. It does, however, require a bit of skill and lots of patience and is not recommended for novice projects.

The easiest type of stencil to use, and the type that is used predominantly throughout this book, is the single-overlay stencil. Single overlay stencils are what most people envision when they hear the word "stencil". The entire pattern is cut from one piece of material. The uncut areas between the design elements are called "bridges" and they are what hold the stencil together, give it strength and help to keep the shape intact. Most precut stencils on the market are cut from either 5mil or 7mil mylar, a durable plastic. The stencils used throughout this book are all cut from a heavier 7mil mylar, which is often blue in color rather than the clear 5mil plastic that thinner stencils are cut from. Thicker stencil material will help you to get a bit higher dimension with your stencil embossing.

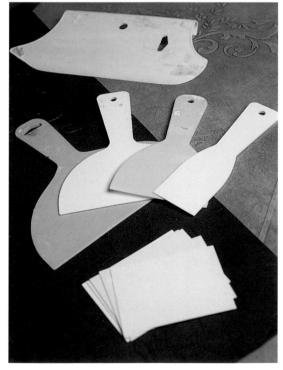

TROWELS

Flexible Plastic Smoothers, designed for wallpaper installation (top), are the ultimate embossing tool for medium to large designs. They are made from soft plastic and have a wide base that curves at the edges. They are ideal for smoothing out lines and applying embossing mediums in large areas. Use a small plastic trowel to load your medium onto the plastic smoother.

Step-by-Step Embossing

Stenciling embossing is a rather straightforward technique that requires more patience and attention to detail than artistic skill. Like any other decorative painting technique, however, you will be best equipped to achieve successful results when armed with detailed information and "insider" tips. This section is offered to provide you with just that. With the addition of some "trial and error" practice you will be off and running to create beautiful embossed effects.

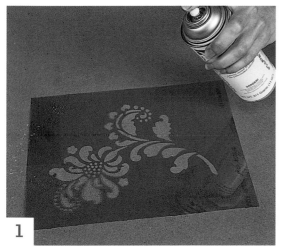

1

Place the stencil face down on a large piece of paper, such as rosin paper or heavy plastic. Holding the can about 12-inch (31cm) away from the stencil, mist lightly and evenly. Allow the adhesive to "set up" for a minute before applying to your surface. Avoid over-spraying, which tends to leave sticky, excess adhesive on your painting surface.

2

Press the stencil firmly down on the surface. Load the trowel (sometimes referred to as "buttering") with a smaller trowel or stick.

3

Hold the trowel at a nearly parallel angle to the surface and gently apply the material through the stencil. This process is much more like icing a cake than spackling a nail hole! If you push too hard you will push a great deal of material under the stencil and may bend or tear the stencil in the process.

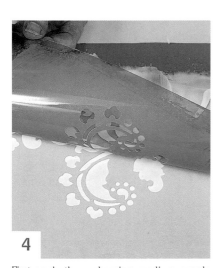

4

First apply the embossing medium evenly and flush with the surface of the stencil, being certain that you have filled it in completely. Remove the stencil at this point if you just desire a low-relief print.

5

If you like more depth, apply more medium. For a higher relief, you'll want an embossed print that is about ⅛-inch thick. Anything higher will begin to get very messy and distorted. Remove the stencil right away.

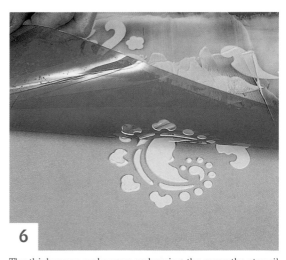

6

The thicker you make your embossing, the more the stencil will pull up little ridges around the edges of the design. These can be sanded down later after the medium has completely dried.

Mistakes and Cleanup

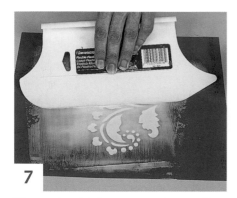

7

8

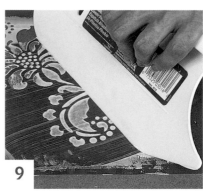

9

When embossing, focus on creating a uniform depth to the material. Otherwise, you could end up with an embossed image that is quite thick in the middle but thin towards the edges. Use a large, plastic smoother to get a "line-free" print. Press from the center of the design out towards the edges to create uniform coverage. Apply enough protective tape around the edges of the design so that you do not "pull up short." Look at the stencil from the side to see if there are areas that are too thick or too thin.

If you find, when you remove the stencil, that your print is not as even as you like, don't panic! When dry, you can either sand down the high spots or replace the stencil and build up more material in the scanty areas. Major boo-boos can be simply scraped away (while wet) and started over!

 TIP

Test to feel if your embossed texture has dried by gently laying the palm of your hand over it. If you feel any coolness, you will know that it has not yet dried completely.

Lay the stencil down on some rosin paper (available at the paint department of your home/hardware store) and scrape off the excess material with a plastic smoother. If the material is still very fresh, you can re-use it. Turn the stencil over and wipe off any excess material with a damp rag or sponge. If necessary, re-spray with adhesive.

FIXING MISTAKES

Inevitably, there will be times when touch-ups will be required. Just accept the fact that this goes with the territory. Joint compound will be the easiest material to remove, as it remains both water-soluble and easily sandable until sealed.

You can try to carefully remove run-unders while the embossed print is still wet. Use a small sharp tool, such as a nail file or stylus. After the embossing has dried, fold fine sandpaper and use it to carefully sand any rough edges.

KEEPING IT CLEAN

Clean embossed prints come from clean stencils. To maintain the quality of your embossing, clean your stencils periodically throughout the project. Stop and clean your stencil if you have had a lot of excess material seep under. Otherwise you will simply be transferring that mess to the wall. Depending on the material you are using for embossing, you may want to stop and clean the stencil every 2–6 repeats.

FINAL CLEANUP

At the end, and perhaps several times during the project, you will want to completely clean your stencil. After scraping off the excess material onto a newspaper or into a bucket, but never into your sink, lay the stencil flat in a sink, tub or on a sheet of heavy plastic. Spray with Simple Green and use a wallpaper brush or foam sanding block to clean both sides of the stencil thoroughly.

Larger stencils can be cleaned on a tabletop covered with plastic. A wallpaper smoothing brush is ideal for scrubbing as it removes all traces of material without bending or damaging the stencil. Clean very large stencils outside with a garden hose.

Pattern Types, Planning & Placement

This useful information on working with various types of patterns is offered here in this chapter on Stencil Embossing. However, these design and layout hints will also apply to traditional stenciling methods.

There are basically three types of patterns used in stenciling: borders, allover patterns and spot motifs. Embossing is a technique that is not rushed. Creating good, clean embossed stenciled prints takes care and time. Choose your patterns wisely depending on your time, budget and your level of patience!

SPOT MOTIFS

Spot motifs will be the easiest type of stencil design to use with the embossing technique. Spot motifs are designs that can be used singularly and separately as focal points on furniture, ceilings and decorative accessories. As an alternative, spot motifs can be repeated to create an allover pattern. The pattern can be a formal and carefully planned grid pattern or a loose random pattern. Either way, using spot motifs to create a repetitive pattern is a less time-consuming choice than a traditional allover pattern because you do not have to worry about any overlap of the stencil over a new, fresh, wet and vulnerable embossed print. This allows you to jump from one print to the next quickly. (See below for tips on creating allover patterns with spot motifs).

Using spot motifs allows you to cover a lot of territory quickly because you do not have to wait for elements to dry. Also, the "open," loose pattern creates the visual impact of an allover pattern with a minimal amount of actual stencil repeats.

Another very positive point to make is that an allover pattern created with the repetition of single motifs can be very dense or very open depending on how closely you decide to space your motifs. You can reduce the amount of time and number of repeats of the pattern by spacing the motifs a larger distance apart while still maintaining the look and feel of an allover pattern. Each project will be different, depending on the size of the motif, the size of the room and the desired finished look. The advantage of using individual stencils to create a unique allover pattern is that you can adapt the design to suit your creative needs.

ALLOVER RANDOM PATTERN IN PROCESS

Here, the pattern has been laid out randomly, yet in a balanced manner. The best way to plan out this type of pattern is to stencil off some quick proofs of the design elements and run off multiple copies on a copy machine. Simply tape the design elements in place on the wall, moving them around until you reach a desirable arrangement. Then replace the copied designs with the stencils as you work across the wall.

LEAP-FROG STENCIL EMBOSSING

When embossing, it is very important not to touch or disturb the raised print while it is still wet. For this reason, you will want to simply go around the room with the border stencil first and JUST trace off the registration marks. When embossing, skip, or "leap-frog" every other repeat of the design. When those repeats have dried, go back and do the "in betweens."

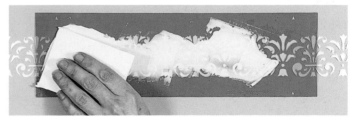

Allover Patterns

Allover patterns are simply stunning when embossed. If you are willing to commit the time it takes to emboss a pattern over a large surface area, you will undoubtedly find that, in the end, the effort was well worth the finished result. One of the reasons that it takes so much time to emboss an allover pattern is because you will be covering every square foot of the treated wall space with the pattern, as opposed to a pattern that is created with individual motifs or borders. Allover patterns also tend to be larger in size and, therefore, a little more unwieldy, particularly when working with the stencil in corners and at the edges.

One of my favorite tricks for eliminating some of these potential issues is to limit the amount of square footage being embossed. Confining the pattern to panels is one of my favorite ways to maximize the artistic impact of stencil embossing on a wall while minimizing the amount of time and effort invested. Another way to "downsize" your wall stenciling project is to limit the allover pattern to the area below a chair rail—or above it.

At any rate, whether you limit it to a defined area or cover a whole room, you will still need to repeat the pattern. As with border designs, you will need to leap frog to different areas of the complete pattern to avoid messing up a freshly embossed print. In order to do this efficiently and precisely, you will need to establish and mark the repeat of the pattern throughout the entire space. There are different types of allover pattern repeats. Some simply use the same types of registration marks as borders. In that case, just lightly transfer the registration marks to the wall through the stencil. More complicated allover repeats can't use those types of marks because the pattern repeats differently in different directions. In that case you may find "window" registrations. In this case, key elements of the design are completely cut through, allowing you to move the stencil and then line up previously painted elements through the open window. Allover patterns can be finished off at corners in ways that not only make them easier to use, but enhance the overall look of the design as well.

Creating panel patterns is a great way to formalize a room and limit the amount of time and energy involved in embossing or stenciling an allover pattern. This follows the "less is more" philosophy. Sometimes a great design or pattern just looks better when it is surrounded by negative space, which sets it off.

Mark the repeat of the allover pattern with "window" registration prior to beginning your project. You can do this by quickly and lightly stenciling in key elements of the pattern. Choose the elements to stencil that are used for registration, rather than taking the time to stencil the whole pattern or stencil quickly (shown) with a glaze.

Space your embossed repeats far enough apart so that you avoid messing up fresh prints with the mylar.

Fill in the remaining repeats after the embossing medium has dried.

WORKING IN CORNERS

Working a stencil design into corners always presents a challenge to stencilers. Trying to emboss a stencil neatly in a tight corner can be aggravating, if not impossible. My strategy is to always look for the easy way!

One great way to finish off borders in a corner is to use a coordinating single motif, such as a tile design, placed at the end of each wall, like bookends! The mylar surrounding the stencil can be trimmed so that it fits snugly in the corner. Mirror the same design on the adjoining wall and treat each corner in the same manner.

Random elements are easy to control. Simply do not place the designs directly in the corners. If you feel that you need to for design purposes, try to find a natural break in the element so that it is easy to do one section on one wall.

FURNITURE

If you are embossing on furniture pieces, cabinetry or any other items or areas that will receive wear, you should use a durable, resin-based medium. Joint compound and spackle-type products are simply not meant to resist chipping, gouging and denting.

BORDERS

Border designs look lovely when embossed, and are really not too difficult to do. The key to success is to pre-plan and mark your registration in advance. Most border stencils include registration marks that allow you to line up a perfect repeat of the pattern. With traditional stenciling you would place your border design, trace through the cutout registration elements to make a light mark on the wall and then stencil. When you move the stencil (right or left), you simply line up the mark that was on the opposite end and continue marking and marching your stencil design around the room.

REMOVING IT LATER

Stencil embossing is a semi-permanent technique. What this means is that it represents something of a commitment. It can be removed at a later date, but not as easily or simply as painting over a previously painted finish.

If you are using a somewhat soft material such as a premixed joint compound on walls, you can chisel it off rather easily and sand it down at a later date. If you are using a more durable marble or resin-based material that is meant to be permanent, you may want to prepare the wall surface for possible later removal. One commonly used method for later removal is to apply wallpaper liner over appropriately sized walls (consult or hire a wallpaper professional), basecoat with an oil-based primer (not water-based, which will loosen the glue) and apply your textural treatment over top of it. The entire treatment can then be removed at a later date by removing the finish along with the layer of wallpaper.

Panels serve many purposes. They create an architectural statement, while limiting the pattern to a defined space. For instance, with this elegant Crewel Embroidery Panel (see page 54) the coordinating gimp braid around the pattern helps to frame it and set it off even more, perhaps, than if it had been stenciled over the entire wall. Gimp braid is available at upholstery fabric stores and can simply be hot-glued in place.

> ✓ TIP
>
> *When stenciling in corners, use a lot of spray adhesive to help hold the stencil flush, and a small application tool to get cleanly into the tight space. You can never do both wall surfaces at one time.*

Faux Fabric Finishes

I HAVE A LIFELONG LOVE OF FABRIC and its possibilities for color, pattern and texture. Some of my best inspiration for painting possibilities comes from trips to upscale upholstery fabric stores. I love to absorb the color combinations, admire the intricate patterns and enjoy the textural quality and feel of the fabrics. In fact, it's hard to go into a fabric store and NOT touch everything! When decorating, the fabrics used can help to set the tone of the room. A silky-smooth, formal damask fabric in a soothing color creates a completely different feeling than a textural, woven fabric with an ethnic design printed in deep, rich colors.

With the help of this book, you can wrap your walls with the look and feel of elegant and unusual finishes that simulate expensive, designer fabrics. Just don't be surprised when people go up and touch your walls!

⟋ TAKE NOTE

For this technique, I have chosen to use "Dead Flat" varnish to stencil the design in a dull finish that will not reflect the light. This type of varnish is designed to protect the finish while creating a completely matte surface. There are other similar types of varnish on the market, but be sure to test them before using on the metallic paint to ensure compatibility. Some varnishes will "frost" over a dark surface.

An alternative to using a flat varnish is to mix the metallic paint color that was used as the basecoat with about 10% flat white latex paint. The larger particles in the latex paint will "kill" the shine while lightening the color slightly. This option creates a little more obvious contrast and may be a better choice for rooms that do not receive a lot of light.

To test how a metallic finish will work in a room, it is best to create a sample board of the desired finish (on poster board or painted polystyrene) and hang it in various spots around the room to see how well it reacts to the available light.

Classic Damask

NAMED FOR THE ANCIENT CITY OF DAMASCUS, where rich patterns were woven in silk, damask fabrics are featured today in many formal decorating schemes. The monochromatic fabric's elaborate patterns are created using a flat weave. It is woven in such a way as to produce a design that shows itself subtly and may even change with the light. That is because the pattern is generally distinguished by a change in the sheen of the fibers which in the patterned area may be silky and shiny while the background is more of a matte finish or vice versa, depending on which side of the fabric you are looking at and how the light is reflecting off of it.

The look of damask fabric is easily created with the combination of simple stenciling and decorative painting techniques and there are many possible alternatives for incorporating this classic, formal look into a design scheme. The tone-on-tone look provides a subtle, quietly textural background that can unify an interior space and provide the ideal understated backdrop for fine furnishings in more formal settings.

SUPPLIES

Royal Design Studio Stencils:

   Allover Interlacing Leaves

   Interlaced Leaves Border

Modern Masters Metallic Paint:

   Venetian Blue

   Sapphire

Modern Masters Dead
Flat Varnish

Modern Masters Extender for
Latex Paint

2-inch (51mm) Easy Mask
paper tape

4-inch (102mm) foam roller
and tray (stenciling)

8-inch (203mm) nap roller
and tray (basecoat)

1-inch (25mm) stencil brush

PREPARATION

This technique is best done on a flat or almost flat wall surface (the bathroom in this project actually had a very light "orange peel" finish on the walls). Basecoat the walls with 2–3 coats of the metallic color. In this case I have mixed equal parts of the two metallic blues to create a custom shade. Add latex extender according to the manufacturer's directions to avoid lap lines.

Use drop cloths to avoid having to clean up over-spray from the roller. Allow the paint to dry for at least 2 days before beginning to stencil.

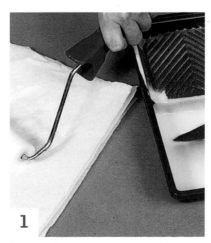

1
Load the foam roller with Dead Flat Varnish from a roller tray. Off-load the excess varnish by rolling a number of times across a stack of paper towels.

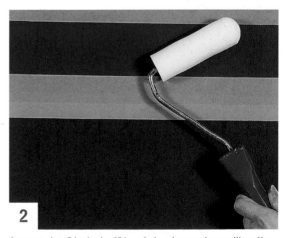

2
I created a 2 1/2-inch (64mm) border at the ceiling line, corners and along the tile with tape. For this demonstration I have created the same size border on the sample by using a ruler and chalk pencil. Easy Mask paper tape works well for creating a nice crisp edge on a smooth surface. If your surface is slightly textured, you should use regular blue painter's tape to create a clean edge. Roll the varnish, using a light, even pressure, in the exposed area between the lines of tape. You will complete all of the border background first and allow the varnish to dry completely.

Classic Damask

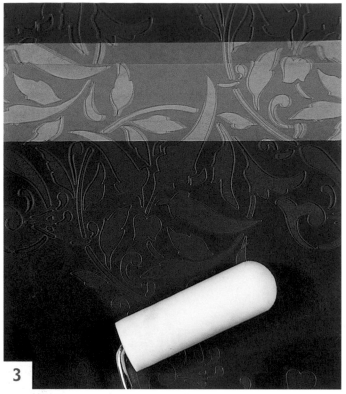

3

Reposition the tape so that it now covers the border area and proceed to stencil the allover pattern on the remaining areas of the wall, using the same roller stenciling method. In a room, you will want to be sure to begin the pattern at the same point at the top edge of each wall.

4

Always lift the stencil right away as you begin a project to be sure that you are using the correct amount of pressure and not getting any seepage under the stencil. As long as you remember to off-load the roller each time after adding more varnish or paint and maintain a light pressure, you will be able to create clean prints. Remember, it is always better to run the roller repeatedly over the stencil opening than to press hard and risk pushing paint under the stencil.

5

Use the mylar surrounding the stencil registration system to align the next repeat. You should be stenciling "dry" enough so that you can immediately go on to the adjoining area. I find it easiest to repeat most allover patterns in vertical rows, beginning at the ceiling line and working down and then either going to the left or right.

6 With the allover pattern complete, go back and simply stencil the border pattern now with the original metallic paint color that was used for the basecoat, using a traditional brush stenciling method.

FINISHED WALL

These photos very effectively show how changing light will affect the way the pattern is seen. With the light straight on, the pattern and background are fairly uniform. By shifting the light to the side you can easily see how the pattern's shiny and dull areas seem to "flip" from the upper right corner to the lower left.

TECHNIQUE 4

Shimmering Silk

HERE IS A VERY SIMPLE FINISH whose beauty lies not only in the fact that it is easy to do, but that it can be adapted to so many design and color variations. There are many different classically inspired allover stencil patterns available that are ideal for a technique of this type. A simple background stria finish behind the stenciling creates a fabric feel and sets the stage for the shimmering metallic stenciled pattern.

As with all metallic finishes, like the previous damask technique, this one changes and adapts with the light source. This means that as the light changes over the course of a day, the look and coloration of the finish will change, allowing you to enjoy a variety of different looks.

> ✎ **TAKE NOTE**
>
> *This romantic finish is ideal for formal rooms, such as bedrooms and dining rooms with good lighting. To see how the finish will look in different lighting situations, prepare a couple of samples on posterboard or polystyrene and hang them at different points around the room prior to painting.*

PREPARATION

Basecoat the walls with two coats of Georgia Pink. Allow to dry a minimum of 2 days.

1

2

3

Mix the Brookline Beige with AquaGlaze at a ratio of 1 part paint to 4 parts glaze. Roll or brush it onto the wall in 2-foot (61cm) vertical sections using long, random strokes. This helps to create unevenness in the depth of color on the stria finish and makes for a more interesting look.

Use the Ultimate Stippler to immediately drag through the glaze and blend the glazed areas together on the wall. Use long, vertical strokes again and a "landing and takeoff" motion on the wall, so that you do not see any indication of where the strokes begin and end. Use a small chip brush or nylon bristle brush for corners, the ceiling line and edges.

Mix a little of the AquaGlaze into the metallic paint (about 1:8 ratio) to use as your stenciling medium. Load the brush as usual but don't off-load as much as you would for traditional stenciling techniques. To keep the vertical lines and fabric look, drag the brush vertically across the stencil opening, as if it were a stria brush. Practice on a sample board to get a feel for the right amount of paint and pressure to use.

4

You should still be able to reposition the stencil right away to continue with the repeat. Don't try to get everything perfect and even. It will add more character to the finish to have a little variety in the depth of color and paint application.

5

A detail of the finished design. Look for inspiration for different color combinations at your local upholstery fabric store, in the fabrics in your house and even in your wardrobe.

TECHNIQUE 5

Batik

BATIK IS AN AGE-OLD METHOD of creating a pattern on fabric by utilizing the principle that wax resists water. It's believed batik was developed in Asia; fragments of batik fabric have even been found in ancient Egyptian tombs. Today, this exotic fabric is created primarily by artists in Bali and Java. Stamps are made of the designs from metal or wood. These stamps are then used to "print" the design onto plain fabric with hot wax. After dying the fabric with water-based dyes in deep, rich colors such as indigo blue, sienna or ochre, the wax is removed, leaving the "resist" pattern.

This is a fairly simple technique for interpreting and re-creating this exotic and somewhat ethnic look for walls. It uses the traditional "resist" concept, but here the resist pattern is applied to a porous, plaster-type wall surface with a stencil rather than a stamp. The wall is then "dyed" with a water-based glaze or stain, revealing a subtle tone-on-tone pattern.

TAKE NOTE   *This "Provence" wall finish features a playful and colorful patchwork of pattern that creates a sunny, casual ambiance. The color and design choices add to the French Country feel. To plan a similar wall treatment, look to the fabrics in your room for color and design cues. Use graph paper and colored pencils to sketch out various possibilities on paper. Your sketches can be used as a blueprint for pattern placement on your walls.*

Royal Design Studio Stencils:

   Large Allover Floral Pattern

   Large Single Floral Pattern

   Provence Olive Border

   Small Scrolling Border

**Benjamin Moore Latex Paints
(MoorGlo Semi-Gloss):**

   Terrapin Green (2145-20)

   New London Burgundy (HC-61)

   Richmond Gold (HC-41)

   Dorset Gold (HC-8)

Behr Sand Texture Paint

satin finish water-based varnish

AquaGlaze

1/2-inch (13mm) nap 8-inch
(203mm) roller and tray

6-inch (152mm) wide plastic
taping knife

wallpaper brush

4-foot (122cm) bubble level

tape measure and pencil

4-inch (102mm) foam roller
and tray

large nylon stipple brush

latex glazing medium

2-inch (51mm) painter's tape

18-inch (46cm) plastic

wide chip brush or
nylon bristle brush

stencil brush

fine-point marker

terry towel

PREPARATION

Applying the Sand Texture paint is a moderately messy job. Protect the ceiling, molding and baseboards with 2-inch (51mm) painter's tape. Additionally, tape 18-inch (46cm) plastic along the baseboards, extending over your dropcloths to protect the floor area. The Sand Texture paint will "shed" gritty sand until it is fully dried and the vertical stria motion with the wallpaper brush will tend to leave excess product at the bottom of the walls. The taped plastic at the floor will catch the mess.

The yellow color is a mix of two parts Richmond Gold with one part Dorset Gold. Mix the paint colors with latex glaze at a ratio of 1 part paint to 3 parts glaze. For a more translucent color, add more glaze. For deeper color, add less glaze. It's always best to experiment and "test" on a prepared sample board. Masonite, 1/8-inch (3mm) thick and cut to 2-foot (61cm) by 2-foot (61cm) squares, is great for making samples using textural products.

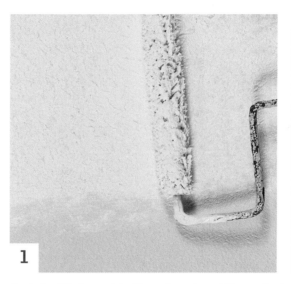

1

Apply Sand Texture paint with a roller or trowel. Use a roller for smooth surfaces and a trowel if the surface has a textured finish. The Sand Texture paint will fill in the underlying texture. Use the trowel at the ceiling line to apply the texture paint evenly and cleanly. Work in 2-foot (61cm) by 3-foot (91cm) wide sections, extending from the ceiling to the floor.

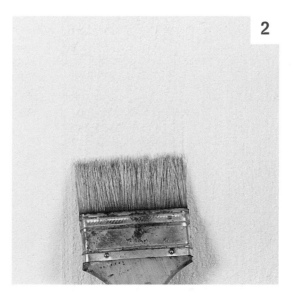

2

With a wide chip brush or nylon bristle brush, lightly drag vertically down through the texture from the ceiling to the floor as you work along the wall. This will smooth out the trowel or roller lines and add a subtle woven look to the finish. The finish should be fairly smooth with just a light texture. Continue around the room. Allow to dry for 24 hours.

Batik

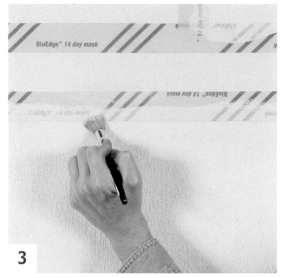

3

Use the tape measure and level to mark off and lightly draw pencil lines delineating the different areas. Tape outside the line and burnish the tape (press it into the surface) to get a good seal. Use a stencil brush to lightly stipple the Sand Texture paint along the edge of the tape. This will further seal the edge of the tape and prevent the glaze from seeping under, leaving a nice clean line.

4

Use the foam roller to roller-stencil the water-based varnish through the stencil. The clear varnish may be a little hard to see, but it does darken the Sand Texture paint slightly. You will be able to see where you have applied it and if you have applied enough. To be sure that you have full, even coverage, pass the roller over the area 2–3 times. Be sure to off-load the roller and use a light pressure on the roller over the stencil. This will help avoid "run-unders" and leave you with a nice clean print.

5

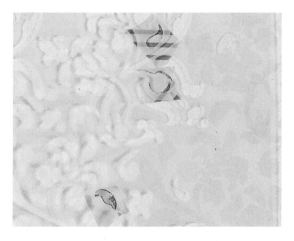

This allover stencil pattern uses a cutout registration method. To help in accurately aligning the next repeat, place tape underneath the cutout registration and trace the element with a fine-point marker. When you reposition the stencil, use these to line it up and then simply remove them before stenciling.

6

Continue in this manner around the room. Be sure that you are getting complete coverage with the varnish, so that your design will fully show up when it is glazed later.

7

After the varnish has dried at least 2 hours, color the area with latex glaze mixed with paint. Mix at a ratio of anywhere from 2–4 parts glaze mixed with 1 part paint. More glaze in the mix will result in a lighter color and more "open" time. Apply the paint/glaze with a chip brush or roller in small areas.

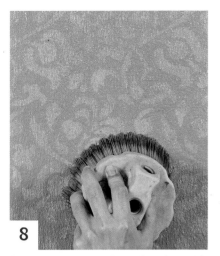

8 Scrub the glaze into the wall surface with a nylon stipple brush. Be careful to apply color all along the edge of the tape without going into the adjoining area. A large stencil brush may be used at the taped edges for better control.

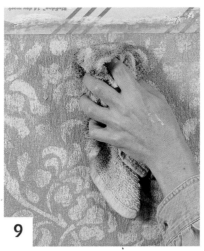

9 Use a damp terry towel to rub excess glaze off the wall and off of the stenciled pattern. You should really see your pattern emerge here—like magic!

10 When your previous area has dried, pull the tape off and re-tape for another area of color and pattern, following steps 3–9. For smaller patterns, such as this border, you may want to use a stencil brush as opposed to a roller.

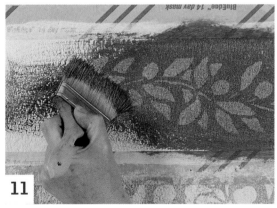

11 With a multi-patterned design like this, plan to work on separate areas of color at one time, i.e., all green vertical borders above chair rail and green allover pattern below. Then go on to the purple-colored areas.

12 Here is a finished detail showing how all of the different colored areas come together.

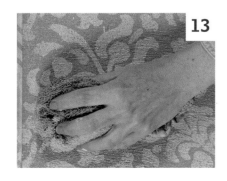

13 If you find it too difficult to see and work with clear varnish, you can try tinting your varnish slightly by adding a small amount of the paint color to it. You will not end up with as much contrast as with the untinted varnish, but it is much easier to see the varnished areas as you are working.

> **✓ TIP**
>
> *Fixing mistakes: If you do need to fix a messy mistake where the varnish has slipped under the stencil, you can simply wipe off the excess wet varnish with a damp cloth. Then reapply the texture paint in that area with a chip brush and try again when it's dry.*

Crewel Embroidery

THIS TECHNIQUE COMBINES TEXTURE upon texture to create the intricate look of an embroidered pattern. After stencil embossing with a textural medium, the design is given a simple stria finish while the stencil remains in place. The result is the look of individual threads within the design.

The textured pattern can then be painted in a variety of ways, depending on the desired look. For the look of traditional crewel embroidery on heavy linen you may even want to add the additional step of creating a textured linen background (see pages 60–63) prior to embossing your pattern. Then choose deep rich colors for your "embroidery."

For a truly magnificent and opulent setting, use shimmering metallic paints to create the elegant look of walls that have been completely "upholstered" in embroidered silk. To downsize the scope of the project, you can create "upholstered panels" on a formal wall by defining and setting off the embroidered areas with the addition of simple wooden moldings. This is also a wonderful effect to use on furniture panels and decorative accent pieces such as picture frames and mirror surrounds.

PREPARATION

Measure and mark out your panels. The placement and size of your panels will be dependent on the wall space and room size you are working with. A 4-foot (122cm) bubble level was used to mark out the lines defining the edges of the panels and 2-inch (51mm) painter's tape was placed outside the lines to define the space and confine the embossed stenciling. Upon completion of all the painting, the gimp braid was glued around the perimeter line.

✓ TIP

I chose to frame these panels with upholsterers gimp braid, both to add to the fabric effect and because it was much easier and less expensive than cutting, nailing and painting real moldings. Simply hot glue the gimp to the wall to create a frame. Decorative wooden moldings would be an excellent addition to this finish if your time, talents and budget allow!

✏ TAKE NOTE

If you are doing this technique with metallic paints, work on a smooth wall surface. Metallic paints are very reflective, and therefore will tend to highlight imperfections in the wall. In order to make this a more manageable project, limit the allover design to formal panels, as shown. This technique isn't limited to allover patterns, of course. Single overlay borders and random elements are ideal as well. Floral and even fruit motifs will work best, as they are often the subject of embroidery designs.

Crewel Embroidery

1 Position the stencil. Stencil spray adhesive, applied to the back, will help to keep the stencil flush with the wall. Larger allover patterns can be heavy and unwieldy. Use tape as well for added insurance that the stencil will stay in place. "Butter" a plastic smoother blade with joint compound. Apply the joint compound over and through the stencil as if you were icing a warm chocolate cake—very lightly and with the blade held almost parallel to the surface. Aim for a very low, even relief, almost just flush with the stencil material.

2 Once you have the joint compound spread out evenly, drag a wallpaper smoothing brush vertically through the material. As with the trowel, hold the smoothing brush at a parallel angle to the surface. Use both hands to ensure an even pressure across the length of the brush.

3 When all embossing has been completed you can easily clean up any minor imperfections or "run-unders." Joint compound is water-soluble and easily sandable until it has been sealed. A piece of fine sandpaper can be used like a file to remove errant joint compound easily. Sometimes even using a fingernail to scrape off unwanted material works wonders. Excess spray adhesive can be removed carefully with mineral spirits. Just be sure to remove anything that is unwanted before painting.

✓ TIP

Remove the stencil carefully and reposition it at a point on the wall where it won't come in contact with fresh, wet embossing and continue. The joint compound should dry enough within 1–2 hours so you will be able to emboss a repeat right next to it. You will see it turn more chalky and opaque. Resist the temptation to put your finger on it to "test" it before it has had time to dry!

4

Paint over the entire area with metallic Champagne using a ½-inch (13mm) nap roller. Add extender according to the manufacturer's directions to create a smoother flow and look to the paint, and to help avoid lap lines. Allow to dry and apply a second and third coat, if necessary. Allow to dry fully, 24–48 hours.

5

Replace the stencil in its original position and use the other metallic paints to create the differing colors within the "embroidery." The way that you color the design is a personal choice. Just be sure to stick with the pattern. Once you establish the coloration on the first repeat it will be easy to follow. Just look at the paint color placement on the stencil and keep repeating it.

6

Here is a detail of the finished design.

Oriental Brocade

THIS EASY BUT VERY DRAMATIC EFFECT uses a simple shift of the stencil with opaque metallic paints to create a small, dark shadow that sets off the metallic design, creating the illusion of brocade fabric. This technique works best on deep rich colors, such as this leather red color. You can also try it on deep blues, greens, eggplant and brown as well as dark metallic basecoats to get equally great results. Instead of gold, consider using silver, bronze, or copper.

It is also a wonderful technique for creating dramatic looks on furniture and fabric and can be used effectively with any single-overlay stencil design.

☞ **TAKE NOTE**

This particular design is a vertical border, meaning that it is meant to run vertically rather than horizontally. So it is perfect for creating a patterned stripe effect on a wall. The addition of the "drop shadow" really sets it off. For balance, the black is picked up in the border at the ceiling line and also in the chair-rail border that divides the stripe pattern from the panel pattern that is created below using the same simple stencil shift.

SUPPLIES

Royal Design Studio Stencil:

   Large Oriental Brocade

   Oriental Brocade Elements

   Laurel Braid

AquaBond:

   Leather Red

   Black

Aqua Dutch Metal:

   Gold

   Silver

¾ inch (19mm) and 1-inch (25mm) stencil brushes

4-inch (102mm) foam roller and tray

stencil spray adhesive

bubble level

chalk pencil

painter's tape

PREPARATION

Basecoat the walls with 2 coats of AquaBond Leather Red. AquaBond is a specialty paint product chosen for its opaque coverage. You could substitute similar colors in the paint line of your choice for the Leather Red and Black.

The Dutch Metal colors are also a unique product in that they are highly pigmented metallic colors that simulate metal leaf, and they pretty much cover in one coat. You can substitute with similar paint products, just make sure that they will provide heavy, opaque coverage.

Use a bubble level and a chalk pencil to mark off vertical lines at your desired width. You can either place the lines so that you will run the design down the wall with it centered over the line or line up the edge of the stencil. Whichever method works for you is the right one!

1

2

Because the stencil will first be painted in a solid, graphic black over many linear feet, you may want to use a roller stenciling technique (page 22) to cover the design area quickly and evenly. Roll using a light, even pressure. Fight the temptation to press hard so you can fill in the areas quickly. A heavy pressure will almost guarantee that the paint will seep under the stencil. You must patiently apply the paint by rolling over the area repeatedly, making sure you get a nice solid print.

After stenciling all the black and cleaning the stencil, you will now go back and stencil everything again in gold. The trick is to shift the stencil slightly and cover most of what you have already put on the wall, leaving just a sliver of black showing as a shadow. To do this correctly, place the stencil directly over the previous stenciling (back in its original position). Now shift the stencil (keeping the same horizontal and vertical lines) up and to the right ⅛-inch (3mm).

Oriental Brocade

You should see the same amount of the red background color exposed on all of the design elements, so check carefully. The amount of red that you see through the stencil will be the same amount of black that will be visible once the second round of stenciling has been completed. Re-stencil the design now with the Dutch Metal Gold. Use a 1-inch (25mm) stencil brush for more control.

This particular paint flows very nicely, and seemingly endlessly, off the brush, so this will go quickly. Be very careful not to have too much paint on the brush, as always. Lift the stencil periodically to check and make sure that you are using the right amount of paint and pressure.

Optional. For a little brighter color, mix 2 parts Dutch Metal Gold with 1 part Dutch Metal Silver to make a Champagne Gold color. Use a ¾-inch (19mm) stencil brush to stipple highlights along the top edges of the design elements.

6 This detail shows a section of the completed Oriental Brocade technique.

7 The panels below the stenciled Laurel Braid chair rail use one of the Oriental Brocade Elements positioned in the corners. Use the same stenciling technique as above. To connect them and finish off the panels, simply measure and tape off 3/8-inch (10mm) wide pinstripes. Stencil them in with a dry brush to get nice clean lines and edges.

TECHNIQUE 8

Printed Linen

THE SUBTLE TEXTURE OF THIS FABRIC finish simulates the fresh and natural look of fine linen. For more than ten thousand years, man has used the fibers of the flax plant to create a fabric that offers a unique blend of comfort and luxury, elegance and practicality. We can now provide the same feeling of relaxed, casual refinement to our walls that we enjoy in our clothing and table linens with readily available paint products, tools and a simple decorative process.

This versatile finish is ideal for creating a subtle, neutral, light textural background in rooms both large and small. Dress it up with real upholstery fabrics in pearlescent, metallic colors of silk, romantic lace or rich velvet. Dress it down with cotton and denim fabrics or more masculine leather upholstered furniture pieces.

An added benefit to this finish is the fact that the textural paint products used to create linen texture can be used to cover and hide the unsightly "orange peel" or "knockdown" wall textures that are used so often these days in new home construction.

PREPARATION

The first layer of Sand Texture paint will effectively cover the entire wall surface. Any existing flat to eggshell basecoat should be fine, as long as the surface is sound (no peeling or chipping) and clean. The texture will also nicely fill in any existing wall texture, such as an orange peel or knockdown finish. You will just need to trowel it on a little heavier.

Premix the Sand Texture paint in a bucket with the Van Buren Brown and mix the Smooth Texture paint with Bone White. Both mixtures should be at a ratio of 1:1 and should be mixed in large buckets with a drill mixer attachment. The paint/texture mix will be runny at first. Allow it to set up overnight or for a few hours before using. Estimated coverage for the Sand Texture mix will be about 100 sq. ft. (9 sq. meters) per gallon and 200 sq. ft. (18 sq. meters) per gallon for the Smooth Texture mix.

This photo shows two types of drill mixer attachments that are available. These are designed specifically for use with heavier textural products and plasters, as opposed to paint.

Prepare the room by carefully taping off at the ceiling and baseboards and along all casings and built in cabinetry. Protect the floor at the edges of the walls by taping a 2-foot (61cm) wide piece of drop cloth plastic around the perimeter of the room along the baseboard line. This could get messy…

✏ TAKE NOTE

This is not a difficult finish to do at all. However, over a large surface area it is recommended that you enlist another set of helping hands. One person can roll or trowel on the texture paint, while the other person follows immediately with the stria brush. If you would like to try this technique on a smaller scale project, consider recessed door panels on cabinetry or furniture—they would be ideal!

Printed Linen

3 Trowel on the Sand Texture mix. Begin at the ceiling line and work from corner to corner across the wall. The trowel makes it very easy to apply the material cleanly into the corners and edges. Move horizontally across the wall, applying about a 2-foot (61cm)–3-foot (91cm) depth of material. Do not apply the material too thickly or your horizontal stria pattern will dominate the final finish too much.

4 Have your helper follow you with the stria brush on a separate ladder to pull horizontal lines through the wet texture mix. Try to keep the lines as level as possible and begin and end each brush stroke away from the wall so that you do not see the start and stop points of the brush. As you move down the wall, simply trowel back in to the previous area slightly and pull the brush through again.

5 When the first layer is completely dry (1 day minimum) apply the Smooth Texture mix. You may choose to trowel this layer on as well, but here I have used a long nap roller to roll on a heavy coat. This layer is worked vertically.

6

Again, apply in vertical areas about 2-foot (61cm)–3-foot (91cm) wide and have a helper follow with the stria brush. You will find that as you pull down you will end up with excess material at the bottom of the wall. Have a bucket handy in which to scrape the excess material off the brush. You will also want to drag up from the bottom to even out the stria.

7

When the linen texture has completely dried, stencil the allover Flourish pattern with the Ultimate Stippler and a paint/glaze mix. Mix 1 part of the Benjamin Moore Brookline Beige with 3 parts AquaGlaze (or similar latex glaze) and use this as your stencil medium. See page 23 for tips on stenciling

8

Add additional color and more vertical movement with an Ultimate Stippler loaded now with a tinted scumble glaze. I used AquaCreme tinted lightly with AquaColor Brown.

9

A detail of the completed linen finish. This technique would work well with many types of allover patterns and even ethnic, floral or botanical motifs!

TECHNIQUE 9

Blue Velvet

RICH AND LUXURIOUS, velvet is a sumptuous fabric that looks equally good dressed up (as in pearls and sparkling gold or silver) or dressed down (as in denim or leather).

The look created here is decidedly dressed up and dramatic. A specialty burnishing metallic plaster in a deep cobalt blue is troweled on in several thin layers and color variations to create incredible depth and dimension. The metallic finish changes with the reflection of the light, just as real velvet does. A random, embossed floral rose adds pattern and plays off the Tango theme.

Try this technique in other deep colors such as bordeaux, emerald, gold and brown to create an elegant look in a dining room, bedroom or master bath suite.

✏ TAKE NOTE

LusterStone is a specialty burnishing metallic plaster that is part of the Gold Label Architectural Coatings line from Faux Effects. It is not inexpensive, but neither does it require a lot of material as it is designed to be troweled on in paper-thin coats.

Working with a trowel comfortably is an acquired skill. I recommend that you purchase some inexpensive sheets of ⅛-inch (3mm) masonite from the home/hardware store to practice on. You can even practice with ordinary premixed joint compound before advancing to the LusterStone material.

Royal Design Studio Stencil:

Large Random Roses

LusterStone from Faux Effects:

Cobalt Blue

Champagne Mist

Benjamin Moore Latex Paint
(Pearl):

Starry Night Blue

black acrylic paint

¼-inch (6mm) nap roller and tray

Venetian trowel

small styrene trowel

1-inch (25mm) stencil brush

low-tack tape for sensitive
surfaces

Scotch-Brite pad

PREPARATION

The wall surface should be smooth. This technique is not suitable for textured walls, which should be skim-coated with drywall mud and primed prior to applying LusterStone. It is recommended that the walls be basecoated with a similar color in a flat or eggshell sheen of a high quality latex paint. The color that I used was Starry Night Blue. This helps to establish a base of the color behind the metallic finish, reducing the number of coats of LusterStone required to gain full color coverage. Allow your base coat to dry for at least 2 days. Tape off along the ceiling, baseboard and molding edges.

1

Thin Cobalt Blue LusterStone slightly (up to 10%) with water. Roll over the entire wall with a short, ¼-inch (6mm) nap roller. Use a stencil brush to stipple the material along edges and in corners. The goal is to provide 100% coverage of material on the wall and provide a "scratch coat" for the following troweled layers to grab on to and bond with. The nap of the roller will create a very low, slight texture.

2

Use a small knife or wood spatula to "butter" the trowel with a small amount of Cobalt Blue Luster-Stone, applying it just along the edge of the trowel that will be your "following" edge. Note that I am left-handed. If you are right-handed, you will butter the opposite side of the trowel.

Blue Velvet

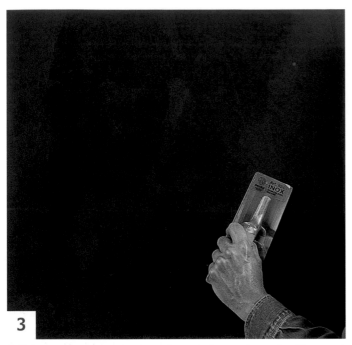

3

Pull the trowel on the surface towards you in long, arcing strokes. The trowel is held almost perpendicular to the surface, with the leading edge just slightly raised. This allows you to apply very thin coats of material. The areas where I am applying the material show up darker blue. Aim for just about 80% coverage on this coat, leaving some irregular open areas. This is the first texture layer. As you apply additional layers over it, the shapes that you set up with the trowel will burnish through, creating a lovely irregular pattern.

4

With any type of plastering technique, it is imperative to maintain a clean trowel. This material dries very quickly and is very durable. Wipe your trowel frequently with a damp towel to remove excess buildup and dried particles. Use a Scotch-Brite pad in a bucket of water to clean stubborn areas. It is also important to keep the material from drying out in the bucket. Keep it covered with a damp towel or simply scoop out small amounts as needed and re-cover.

5

Apply a second texture layer of Cobalt Blue LusterStone. This layer will be applied the same as the first and will fill in any uncovered areas as well as creating a second layer over most of the previous layer. While applying this layer, you can start to "burnish" the material by pressing harder on the edge of the trowel. The harder you press, the more the material will shine and the more the underlying layer will show through.

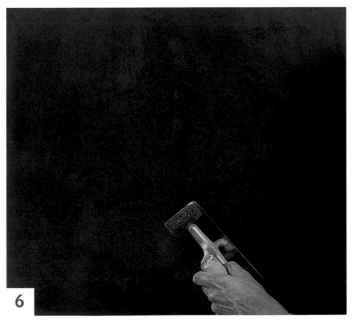

6

If desired, a third layer can be applied. The more layers that are applied, the greater the depth and shine created (with the finish). Prior to applying this layer, take the clean trowel and simply burnish the wall by dragging across it in long, arcing strokes.

7

For the final layer, mix the Cobalt Blue LusterStone 1:1 with Champagne Mist LusterStone. This will lighten the color slightly, and when applied, will create more depth as well as the look of a velvet nap that has had a hand run across it.

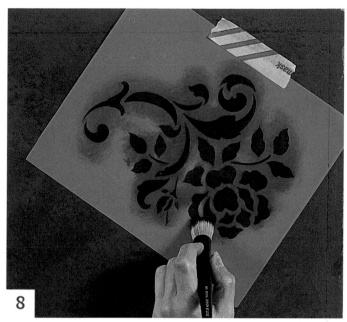

8

I chose a random rose pattern to finish off this wall. See pages 39–40 for tips on laying out and working with patterns. This stencil technique uses three different shades of the same color, along with a simple stencil shift, to create a highly interesting, dimensional look. First, mix a small amount of Cobalt Blue LusterStone with black acrylic paint to darken at a ratio of 1 table-spoon Cobalt Blue to ¾ teaspoon black acrylic. Thin the mixture slightly with water and stencil normally, using the swirling, dry-brush method. Complete all of this color around the room.

9

Go back and hold the stencil in its original position and then simply shift the entire stencil up and to the right about ⅛-inch (3mm) or slightly less. It is important to always shift the stencil in the same amount and in the same direction. You will know that you have it shifted evenly if all of the areas of newly exposed base color are equal.

Blue Velvet

10 Mix some Cobalt Blue LusterStone now 1:2 with Champagne Mist LusterStone to create a lighter value of blue. Use a small, flexible styrene trowel to apply a thin layer of the mixed LusterStone. Hold the trowel very flat to the surface and use a light pressure to avoid pushing material under the stencil.

11 Before removing the stencil, stipple the area lightly with a stencil brush to create a slightly nappy texture.

12 The stippled rose print.

Finally, mix plain Cobalt Blue LusterStone with about 10% water. Replace the stencils in their original position (where you originally stenciled the darkest blue). Stencil over again with the thinned Cobalt Blue, using the traditional dry-brush stenciling technique.

This detail clearly shows the three distinct values of blue, creating a dramatic highlight, midtone and shadow effect.

A detail of the final illusion.

Taking Stenciling to New Heights

STENCIL EMBOSSING is one of the most exciting and versatile techniques available for creating artistic illusions. We have already explored some great options for stenciled embossing treatments. But we have only just begun to scratch the surface. There are a multitude of options for adding additional paint treatments to the raised design to create the illusion of a variety of different surfaces. With many different paint and textural treatments, you can create the look of expensive materials and architectural accents for your home.

📖 **TAKE NOTE** *Leather today comes in many colors. Besides the color combination presented here, consider deep red, green or even blue. If you wish to stick with the neutral color family, you can also try a darker brown—or go lighter with a yellow ochre basecoat.*

Because the embossed design will be covered and sealed with the combination of tissue paper and paint, it will be fine to simply use premixed joint compound as your embossing material.

Embossed Leather

FOR A WARM, STATELY LOOK NOTHING COMPARES TO LEATHER. Combine a stencil embossing technique with an easy painted and glazed tissue-paper finish and you can create the elegance of embossed leather for yourself. This technique is an ideal one to incorporate in rooms that are decorated in a more masculine style, such as libraries and studies. And it can be done on walls, doors and decorative furniture pieces. It also provides a wonderful opportunity for creating artistic "accents" in more casual rooms and can be used on floor screens, recessed panels, lamp bases and cornice boxes.

SUPPLIES

Royal Design Studio Stencils:

  Micah

  Small Sophistiscroll

AquaSeal

AquaBond:

  Camel

AquaStain & Seal:

  Rich Brown

AquaGlaze

premixed joint compound

stencil spray adhesive

assorted trowels

tissue paper (packaging type)

½-inch (13mm) nap roller and tray

medium-grit foam sanding block

old paintbrush

nylon stipple brush

3-inch (76mm) chip brush

3-panel screen from Scumble Goosie (see Resource Guide)

PREPARATION

To do the project as shown, you will want to carefully measure and mark the placement of the stenciled border before beginning. The arched screen is made from masonite. There is no need to prime it before beginning. The small border design is placed ½-inch (13mm) in from the sides and bottom and 4-inches (102mm) down from the arched top. The center design repeats itself down the middle of each panel and is centered inside the border area.

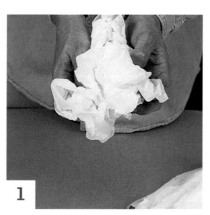

1 Pre-crumple the tissue before beginning and lay it out in a stack. Note: Some people prefer to tear the overlapping edges to avoid having a straight edge that shows through the finish where the pieces of tissue paper meet.

2 Emboss the designs according to the techniques and instructions laid out in Chapter 3. Aim for even coverage throughout, approximately ¼-inch (6mm) thick. Allow to dry completely.

3 Lightly sand down any ridges or rough edges. A foam sanding block helps to create an even finish. Take care to just sand down the imperfections. Don't get too carried away and sand off all of your dimension.

Embossed Leather

Roll on the AquaSeal (or substitute a water-based varnish), covering an area just a little larger than your sheet of tissue paper. It is imperative to get 100% coverage with the AquaSeal. Otherwise, the tissue paper will have nothing to bond to and you will end up with bubbles in your finish.

4

Remove all excess dust with an old paint brush. Better (and cleaner) yet, just use the dusting attachment on your vacuum cleaner.

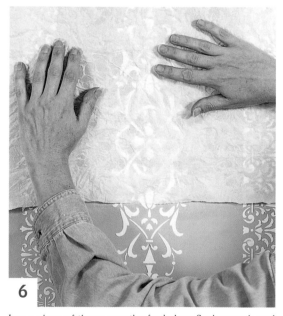

6

Lay a piece of tissue over the fresh AquaSeal; smooth and flatten it slightly by patting down on it with the palms of your hands. Try to find a happy medium between heavy wrinkles and a predominantly flat surface. Pat with a straight up and down motion.

7

Immediately apply another layer of AquaSeal. You will be sealing the textured tissue paper between two coats of AquaSeal. Use the roller to push out air bubbles (if any) towards the edges of the tissue. Use a firm pressure over the embossed areas, in particular, to ensure a tight seal of the tissue paper and to accentuate the raised images.

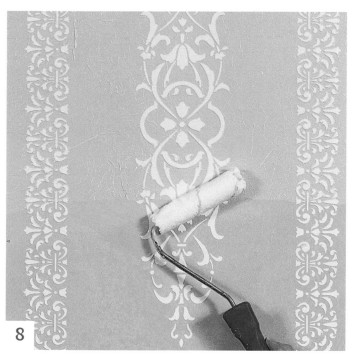

8

Apply the next section of tissue in the same manner. Roll on a generous coat of AquaSeal, place the tissue and press, then smooth it. Allow only a slight overlap of the tissue. If the tissue has too much overlap and thickness over the embossed areas, you will lose some of your dimension. It will get buried under tissue. Be sure to seal the overlapping edges well.

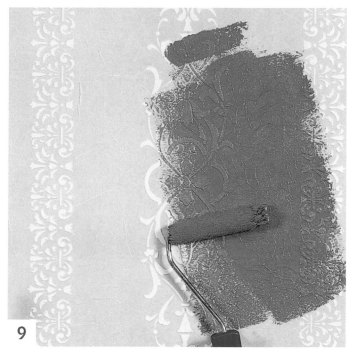

9

When the initial sealing layer is dry, basecoat the area with two coats of AquaBond Camel, or a latex satin paint of a similar color. Dry thoroughly.

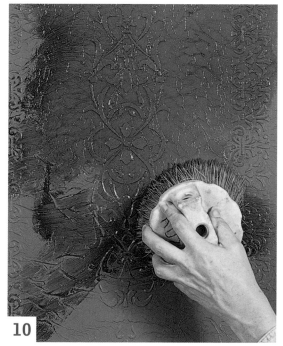

10

Mix Rich Brown AquaStain & Seal, a water-based gel stain, with some AquaGlaze at a ratio of 1:3. Apply with a chip brush to small areas, and swirl and scrub the stain into the tissue finish with a nylon stipple brush.

11

After the stain/glaze has set up just slightly (a few minutes), use the palm of your hand to burnish the glaze into the tissue. This will accentuate the tissue and the raised stencil texture. You will also create the look of pores in the final finish, adding to the illusion of real leather.

Porcelain Crackled Tile

THIS IS A GREAT LOOK FOR A BACKSPLASH in a bathroom and/or kitchen. There are many stencils available that are designed specifically to create tile looks. This rose and scroll motif is unusual because it doesn't fit into a square pattern. But it adds nice movement and curvilinear lines to the dominant squares and right angles of the tiles.

📇 TAKE NOTE *Whenever you create a decorative finish in an area that will be subject to a lot of cleaning, such as a kitchen or bath, you will want to protect it well from scrubbing sponges and harsh chemicals. Roll on 2–3 layers of a good quality water-based top coat after the finish has completely dried and cured.*

PREPARATION

Mix up a small quantity of "Royal Plaster" (about one quart at a time.) The plaster works best when used within the first two days of mixing, so don't mix a lot up in advance. The surface to be "tiled" should be smooth and sound (no chipping or peeling paint) and cured.

Use a grid ruler to carefully measure out and mark your tile design. The size of the tiles is arbitrary, meaning it is up to you. The size tiles you choose will be dependent on the size of the decorative design that goes on them and on the dimensions of the area you wish to decorate. For instance you wouldn't necessarily want to place 12-inch (31cm) tiles in a 2-foot (61cm) by 2-foot (61cm) space because the scale of the tiles would be too big. The tiles created for this project are 6-inch (152mm) squares. When you are planning, remember to include the width of the grout line, which is 1/8-inch (3mm), in the measurements.

1 Run 1/8-inch (3mm) tape down the center of the pencil lines. Pull the tape taut enough to keep it straight but be careful not to pull the tape into a thinner width. Burnish the tape (rub it tight onto the background) as you go with your fingernails or a piece of stiff plastic (such as a credit card).

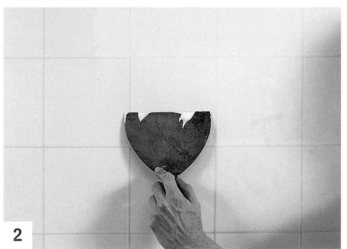

2 Use a metal taping knife to apply the "Royal Plaster" (see page 35) in a smooth thin coat over the entire surface. It may be helpful to pull down the middle of the tile rows. Your material should only be applied about 1/16-inch (1.6mm) thick. This will not be a high relief. If it gets too thick, you will bury your tape and it will be almost impossible to remove. Once your plaster is dry, sand down any ridges or imperfections. Wipe with a damp cloth and apply another thin coat of plaster. Sand down and wipe again.

Porcelain Crackled Tile

Emboss your tiles with the same "Royal Plaster" mixture, building up the design to about a ⅛-inch (3mm) thickness. I have chosen to place the same rose motif in alternating tiles. I use a black permanent marker to draw lines on the stencil indicating the edges of the tiles. This ensures that each rose motif will be placed in the same spot in each tile.

Remove the tape. You will re-tape later. It is best to remove the tape at this layer so that it doesn't get buried, which makes it extremely difficult to remove.

4

Sand again, paying particular attention to the edges of the tiles and the embossed motifs. Wipe thoroughly with a damp cloth to clean off all the dust.

5

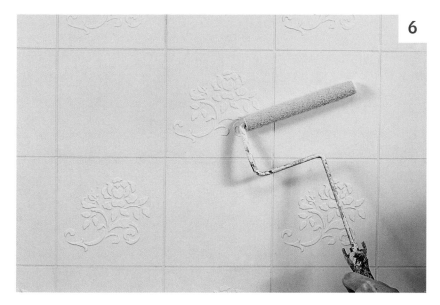

6 Base coat the entire area with a water-based latex primer. This will act as a primer/sealer for the Royal Plaster. Allow to dry thoroughly.

Re-tape the entire design area, carefully laying the tape straight and in the grooves that were created with the tile embossing. Press the tape firmly to the surface with something small, like the edge of a pencil eraser.

7

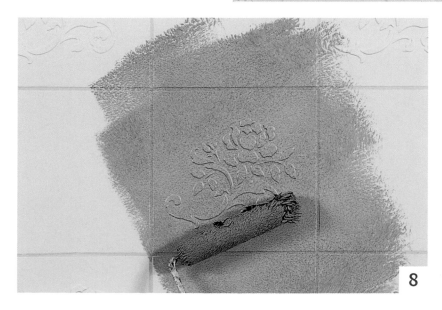

8 Base coat further with two coats of Modern Masters Sage and Pearl White, which have been mixed together at a ratio of 1:1. Add a small amount of Modern Masters Latex Extender, according to manufacturer's directions, to reduce lap lines and create a smooth finish. Allow to dry.

Porcelain Crackled Tile

9 With a clean, fresh roller apply the crackle size in a smooth, even coat by rolling in one direction. Allow to dry for 30 minutes. Apply a second coat, now rolling in the opposite direction. Applying two coats of size will ensure 100% coverage of the size and even crackling.

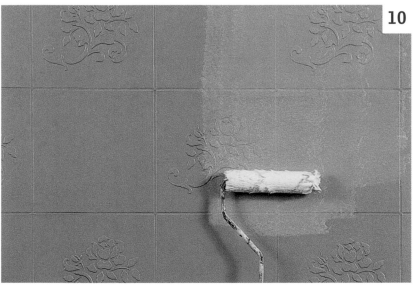

10 After the size has been allowed to dry approximately 30 minutes, use a fresh roller to roll on a generous, even coat of China Crackle Medium. This will dry clear and crack in about two hours. It will be very hard to see the cracks until you apply the deep toning layer in the next step.

11 Create a loose wad with a piece of cheesecloth and dip it into the Modern Masters Crackle Enhancer. Rub it into the finish to expose and accentuate the cracks. Use another piece of dampened cheesecloth to wipe off the excess. Allow to dry.

12 To the metallic Pearl White paint, add Modern Masters Latex Extender (a quantity of 25% of the total amount of Pearl White paint). Use another piece of fresh cheesecloth to rub it over the entire surface. This will lighten the finish and the pearlescent finish will catch the light and help to enhance the embossing.

13 The tape will have many layers of paint over it at this point, so use a sharp craft knife to carefully score the lines before pulling the tape. A ruler may be helpful in keeping the lines straight.

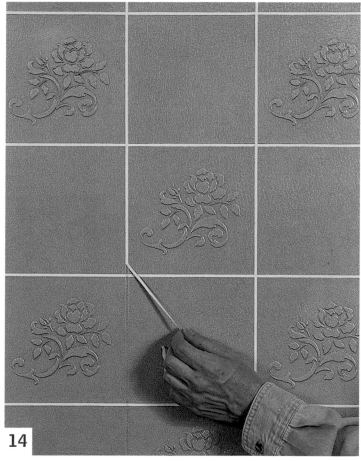

14 Pull off the tape slowly and carefully to be sure you are getting a clean line.

Creativity without Carpentry

THIS CHAPTER FEATURES TROMPE L'OEIL projects that simulate the look of expensive wood—marquetry, fine wood and expensive carved detailing. It is hard to find the kind of wood craftsmanship and detailing in today's homes that were common a century ago. Fine wood treatments are expensive and rare. Fortunately, they are also easy to reproduce with simple paint and stain treatments. You can adapt the following techniques to almost any wood surface in your home—real or "faux."

> **TAKE NOTE** *Because of the simplicity of this technique, it would be a great quick and easy finish for smaller wood areas such as crown moldings, shelves, cabinet doors, frames and more.*

Faux Oak Paneling

THERE ARE MANY WONDERFUL REFERENCE MATERIALS for creating highly detailed and involved renderings of different types of exotic woods. This is not one of those. This is a faux wood technique born out of frustration, impatience and a total lack of time—but it works!

Half the battle of producing a decent illusion is getting the right colors nailed down and then finding the tools that will produce a texture that hints of the original.

Because this paint illusion is designed as a background for some stenciling (coming later) it is intentional that the resulting wood finish remains simple and non-competitive. This is not necessarily meant to be a stand-alone finish, simply a great background that is part of an even greater illusion.

SUPPLIES

AquaBond:

  Camel

Aqua Stain & Seal:

  Rich Brown

AquaGlaze

faux wood graining "rocker" tool

flogger specialty brush

3-inch (76mm) chip brush

bubble level

PREPARATION

Basecoat the surface with AquaBond Camel or a similar latex paint color in a satin finish. Dry a minimum of two days. This project requires a water-based wood stain. Because it is a stain, the color is very intense and rich. Since it is water-based, it is designed to dry very quickly. Add one part AquaGlaze to the stain to give it glaze-like properties and increase your working time.

Predetermine the width of your panels. Not only does limiting the width of the panels create a more realistic look, it also provides a smaller, more workable area. For the project as shown, the width of the faux wood panels is 26-inches (66cm).

Measure and tape off panels using a bubble level and light pencil line. You will create your wood grain illusion in every other one, so place the tape accordingly. Let the panels dry overnight, then reposition the tape to the other side of the line and repeat the process.

Brush or roll on glaze vertically. A 3-inch (76mm) chip brush is perfect for these smaller areas, and helps to establish the grain.

Smooth out by dragging from top to bottom and bottom to top with the brush. Try to use very vertical brush strokes (straight up and down).

Faux Oak Paneling

3 This wood graining "rocker" tool takes some getting used to, so practice on a painted sample board first. Start at the top and pull straight down slowly, in a very controlled manner. As you pull down you will "rock" the roller slightly forward and then backward. Different speeds of rocking will produce different patterns. Aim for a variety of different looks and lengths of the concentric elongated circles.

4 Drag very lightly again with a chip brush to slightly soften out the obvious grain.

✓ TIP

On a real wall application, where your paneling is along the floor, you will need to bend forward with your back to the wall and work down!

5 The flogging brush will further soften and smooth out the graining, while adding the look of elongated pores that are indicative of oak. Begin at the bottom and work up. Hold the brush very flat and parallel to the wall and "slap" the wall with very short strokes. As you lift the brush, allow it to come away from the wall just enough to move it forward.

6 Soften slightly again, lightly dragging over the surface with the chip brush. Always brush in the direction of the grain.

✓ TIP

While this technique is shown on the faux oak finish, it is also very successful when done on real wood or on other types of background finishes, such as painted faux marble, granite and limestone.

7 The finished faux oak graining.

Decorative Carved Dado

THIS IS AN INCREDIBLY EASY AND EFFECTIVE illusion that takes full advantage of the unique properties that stencil painting offers. The illusion of a carved surface is achieved by the use of a simple, single overlay stencil design. In this case, the stencil used is a "negative" stencil design. What this means is that the negative spaces, or the areas directly surrounding the actual design, are cut out of the stencil material. These negative areas are then carefully shaded and defined using the basic dry-brush stencil technique which produces a fade-away effect. The light source is established, in most cases, as coming from above. Deeper shading at just the top edges of the "carving" helps to enforce the illusion.

You can utilize this technique on wooden panels, crown molding, decorative boxes, tiles and mantels. All that is required is a "negative" stencil pattern and attention to shading, which will interpret the effect of light and shadow on a carved surface.

Decorative Carved Dado

PREPARATION

For the paneling application shown here, I decided not to stencil the pattern as a continuous border. Instead, I chose to break it up into smaller panels. This not only added architectural interest, it also saved some stenciling time!

Tape off areas within the panels that are 22-inches (56cm) wide. The height of the panels shown, excluding the baseboard, is a total of 31-inches (79cm). I have placed the stencil design 4-inches (10cm) from the top and bottom.

SUPPLIES

Royal Design Studio Stencil:

Carved Arch Panel

Aqua Stain & Seal:

Van Dyke Brown

Ebony

1-inch (25mm) stencil brush

½-inch (13mm) stencil brush

1

Stencil the design first with the Aqua Stain & Seal Van Dyke Brown. Do not thin the stain for stenciling—it is the perfect consistency right out of the container. "Hug" the edges of the stencil openings, building up a nice crisp depth of color around the edges that will fade to nothing in the centers. It will be difficult to do this in the smaller areas unless you switch to a much smaller brush.

2

Here is the completed design using just one color. You can see that the stencil shading is very effective for creating a variety of values, which gives the illusion of a carved surface.

3

To add even more contrast and "pop" to your illusion, go back with a smaller brush and Aqua Stain & Seal Ebony. Because we are imagining that the light source is coming from above, the shading is focused on only the upper areas of the carved design. These are the areas that would receive the least amount of light if this design were actually carved into the surface.

4

Lift the stencil often while you are working to see the true effect of your painting. When the stencil is in place, it can be deceiving as to how much color you are actually applying.

5

Here is a detail of the finished illusion of carved paneling. It's amazing how easy and effective this illusion actually is!

TECHNIQUE 14

Faux Marquetry

INTARSIA IS AN ITALIAN FORM of marquetry in which thin wood pieces of varying sources and hues are carefully cut and used to create a decorative pattern or design. It is a time-consuming process that is practiced by master craftsmen and is very costly. Fortunately, the illusion of inlay to a floor or piece of furniture is very easy and inexpensive to reproduce with a simple multi-overlay stencil.

This technique is ideal for wood floors, furniture panels, tabletops, wide crown molding and shelves.

You will want to carefully choose the type of wood and the type of stencil design for this project. The wood should have a simple graining pattern and be completely free of knots and imperfections. Alder and poplar are good choices, as is oak which has a tight grain. A simple, graphic stencil design of two or three overlays, with little or no small details, is the best design choice here.

PREPARATION

This technique uses water-based gel stains. These are more desirable than oil-based stains, in my opinion, because of the lack of odor, ease of cleanup and quick drying time. If you prefer to work with oil, however, the stenciling technique will be basically the same.

On new wood surfaces, sand the surface lightly with fine sandpaper. You may want to first apply a sanding sealer. This medium will seal the surface slightly and help to create a more even finish when the stain is applied. Whether you start with sanding sealer or water-based stain, you will find that it will raise the grain of the wood slightly. This should be lightly sanded down and wiped with a tack cloth before stenciling and finishing.

On previously finished wood surfaces, simply sand over the area lightly with fine sandpaper to break the surface and provide some "tooth." Stencil in the same manner as detailed in the following steps. After the stenciling has completely dried and cured, recoat with several layers of the same topcoat that was previously used. In effect, you are sealing the stencil layer between layers of finish coats. You will find that you will need very little stain on the brush when working on a sealed (finished) surface as opposed to a raw, porous one.

1

This project is shown on a piece of precut oak that was purchased from a home supply or hardware store. The same basic technique can be applied to all wood surfaces. Apply a thin layer of Aqua Stain & Seal Rich Brown to the raw wood with a foam or chip brush. Because the Stain & Seal is water-based, it tends to dry very quickly, which can be a problem over large surface areas. I like to add 25% to 50% AquaGlaze to the stain to make it more translucent and extend the open time. This allows for a more even finish.

✏ **TAKE NOTE** *Instead of the traditional stencil shading that is done to visually separate the different elements within the design, these elements will be defined by using different shades of stain. Therefore, you will want to choose your colors and plan your pattern carefully, since you will want slightly different shades of colors to be placed side by side. A design containing two or three overlays is ideal. Also, choose classic, architectural designs as these would be the types of designs most often used in real marquetry and intarsia.*

Faux Marquetry

2

Wipe off the excess glaze with a piece of cheesecloth. Before stenciling, it is always best to start with a thin layer of stain on raw wood. Otherwise the stain will absorb too quickly and darkly into the wood when stenciling. When staining, the more layers you apply, the richer the final look.

3

You will find that the water-based stain will raise the grain of the wood. Sand it lightly with fine, finishing sandpaper. Always work in the direction of the grain of the wood, whether you are staining or sanding.

4

Remove all surface dust with a tack cloth. This is a specially treated piece of cheesecloth that is sticky. Store it in a plastic bag to protect it from dirt and from drying out.

5

Stencil overlay no. 1 of the design with Aqua Stain & Seal Antique Mahogany. Do not add AquaGlaze to the stain that you will use for stenciling. If you want the stain to thicken and work even better for the stenciling technique, leave a small amount of the stain uncovered overnight. Stencil with the dry brush method, but finish off each element by taking the stencil brush and brushing in the direction of the grain.

6

Apply small pieces of painter's tape under the areas of the repeat registration marks and make your marks directly on them. This will help to avoid marking the wood surface.

7

After finishing all of overlay no. 1, stencil no. 2 in Aqua Stain & Seal Van Dyke Brown. You may find that you want to stencil each overlay twice to get the depth of color desired. If the color builds up slightly in the lines around the edges, that's fine. That will just add to the illusion.

8

Border designs look great when finished off with banding stripes. Use your grid ruler to mark light lines and place paper tape to create a clean, straight edge. Stencil as above, swirling and then dragging along the direction of the grain lines.

9

You can see what a nice clean edge the paper tape leaves.

Seal and protect your wood surface with multiple coats of a good-quality, water-based satin varnish.

CHAPTER
7

An Assortment of Illusions

THERE ARE MANY TYPES OF ILLUSIONS. A painted illusion can be anything that represents an artificial sense of reality with paint, pattern, shading and sleight of brush. Illusions can be big or small, simple or complex. What they all have in common is that they entertain and delight the viewer, enhance the space and provide the "do-er" with a great sense of satisfaction and joy.

🖎 **TAKE NOTE**

There are hundreds of different color options for this technique. Study some real granite samples or pictures for more ideas. Remember that while painting this technique, your dominant color will be sponged on first. The colors that you want to appear only as small flecks will be sponged and rolled on afterwards.

Gold-Inlaid Granite

SUPPLIES

Royal Design Studio Stencil:

Small Ornamental Rose

Corner

Modern Masters Metallic Paints:

Copper Penny

Ivy

AquaBond:

Black

¼-inch (6mm) tempered glass, cut to size

white adhesive shelf paper

Air-O-Size

rubbing alcohol

cotton swabs

sea sponge

Easy Leaf adhesive spray

composition gold leaf

1-inch (25mm) stencil brush

paper towels

painter's tape

craft swivel knife and extra blades

pick knife

dense foam roller

single-edge blade in safety holder

GRANITE, AN IGNEOUS ROCK WITH VISIBLE CRYSTALLINE TEXTURE, is a very popular option for counters and tabletops. It comes in hundreds of different color variations and can complement almost any décor. It is a popular decorative finish choice. It is very easy to simulate by sponge painting various colors in a tight, overlaying pattern.

This technique uses sponge painting, but with a twist. The painting is done in reverse on glass. When the painting is finished and the glass is turned over, it imparts a depth and shine that creates a more realistic "illusion granite" than can ever be achieved by traditional painting methods. For fun, and to add more design and interest, I have added a gold inlay design to the project as well.

1 Use white adhesive shelf paper to completely cover the glass surface. In order to avoid a sticky mess, apply the shelf paper carefully. Peel back one edge and smooth the paper onto the glass. Slowly and carefully pull the paper towards you with one hand as you smooth and secure it to the surface with the other hand or with a plastic trowel. For large areas you may have to piece the shelf paper. Overlap the edges slightly to ensure complete coverage.

2 Stencil the desired design directly on the shelf paper. I find it helpful to create stenciled proofs of the design I am planning. Use them as a guide to try out different placement options.

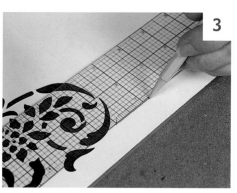

3 This particular project includes a gold pinstripe that connects the motif that is placed in each corner. This is simply drawn in with a pencil and grid ruler.

Gold-Inlaid Granite

Cut out the design using a craft swivel knife. This knife has a very small blade that swivels in the base; you (and the surface you are cutting) can stay in the same position while the blade does all the work of moving. Keep the blade on the cutting surface and just allow it to swivel to turn corners and angles. It does take a little getting used to, so I suggest you practice a bit first. Also, change your blade as soon as it begins to dull. It is very difficult to cut well, or safely, with a dull blade.

Use a pick knife (a separate specialty tool) to lift out each design element as you go. Place the knife in the middle of the element, spear through it, and lift off. When completed, clean off any excess adhesive that has been left on the glass with a small amount of alcohol on a paper towel.

Spray the entire area lightly with Air-O-Size. Lift glass to look through to a light source to ensure that you have gotten full coverage. Spray just enough to cover. Allow the size to set up for a minute or two.

The gold leaf will come in a "book" and each piece will be separated by tissue paper. To remove easily, simply roll back the rest of the book to expose a piece of leaf.

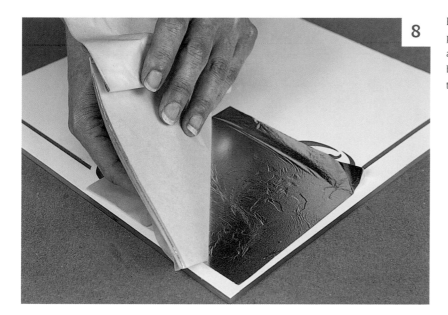

8 Roll the exposed piece of leaf over the design area as you pull back the tissue. You will need to overlap the leaf in areas to get it to cover. For smaller areas, you can also cut the book into small pieces. You can also simply use your hands to place smaller pieces of leaf where you need them.

Use a stencil brush with a swirling motion to tamp the leaf down and burnish it into all of the edges of the cutout design.

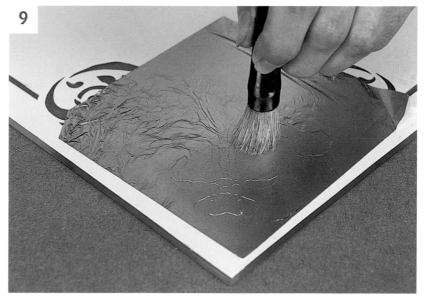

9

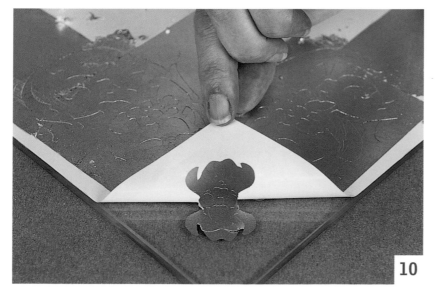

10

Carefully pull away the shelf paper. The leaf will stick where you have sprayed. When the shelf paper is removed, it will remain only in the design area. You will have to use the pick knife again to remove many of the bridges between the design, as the shelf paper will tear in weak areas as you remove it.

Gold-Inlaid Granite

11 Use alcohol again on a paper towel to carefully remove any excess residue of adhesive on the glass. A cotton swab is helpful for getting into tight spaces.

12 Use a damp sea sponge to dab on unthinned black paint, leaving open areas. Test different sponges; the best type for this project will leave larger, uneven areas of paint as opposed to prickly little dots of color. Many times I will use the back side of the sponge as opposed to the more textured top side. Allow the black paint to dry.

13 This piece of glass is lifted up to show how much of the glass was covered with the sponged-on black paint. If you want to end up with more or less of the other colors showing through, adjust your sponging accordingly.

14

Randomly sponge on Metallic Copper Penny, still leaving some open areas. Hold the glass up to the light again to see the results you are getting. It is hard to see the effect when the glass is lying down on a table top. Allow this paint layer to dry.

15

Use a dense foam roller to apply an even coat of Metallic Ivy. This is the color that shows through the least, as most of the glass surface will have already been covered up by the black and copper. Carefully clean up any paint residue that may have gotten on the edges of the glass with a single-edge razor blade mounted in a safety holder. Allow the multiple layers of paint to dry completely (2 days minimum) before placing on your table or dresser.

A detail of the finished gold inlaid granite.

Faux Stone Tile

CREATING FAUX STONE TILES and blocks is a classic illusion. It is an easy and inexpensive way to create "instant architecture" on walls and floors. The beauty of this technique is that it is appropriate for almost any design setting and can be adapted to many different variations of scale. Depending on how you initially plan, measure and place the tape, you can create allover schemes or simply create stone and tile archways, pediments, cornices or walls.

There are many different painting and textural techniques that have already been presented elsewhere. I now add this very simple and effective method to the long list of options for creating stone tile and block.

☞ TAKE NOTE

The size and scale of the stone tiles that you create will be determined by the context and location where they will be used. For this decorative dado design, I considered using much smaller tiles, but in the end opted for these large 181/2-inch (47cm) squares. There were two main reasons: First, I thought that smaller tiles would end up looking too busy and would compete with the "carved" stenciled border. Second, going with larger tiles certainly cuts down on the amount of taping required!

To plan your project, get some graph paper and transfer the measurements of your project area to scale. Then, sketch out your various options. You'll have a great reference for measuring and taping as well as a visual that reveals what your final results will look like.

When you turn squares on their sides they become diamonds. Be aware that the diagonal measurement from point to point will be greater than the size of the square, which is determined by measuring from corner to corner. So a 12-inch (30cm) square turned on its side will now measure 17-inches (43cm) each way. You can roughly figure out the difference by multiplying the size of the square by 1.41 to get the measurements for a diamond. Conversely, if you know that you want your diamonds to measure 261/4-inches (67cm) across, as I did for this project, you simply divide that number by 1.41 to determine the size of the squares.

PREPARATION

The background wall surface should be flat to only slightly textured for this finish. Clean the surface well with trisodium phosphate before repainting to remove all grime, grease and dust. Basecoat the wall with two coats of Linen White (or a similar color) in a semi-gloss finish. Allow to dry and cure for a minimum of two days or up to two weeks. You need to take care, particularly when executing a finish that involves tape, to ensure that the basecoat is sound and completely dry. Otherwise, you will run the risk of pulling the paint off with the tape.

Mix Fairview Taupe and Berkshire Beige separately with AquaGlaze. The ratio of paint to glaze should be 1:4.

SUPPLIES

Benjamin Moore Paint
(AquaPearl):

   Linen White

   Fairview Taupe (HC-85)

   Berkshire Beige (AC-2)

AquaGlaze

1/8-inch (3mm) tape
for grout lines

sea sponge

terrycloth rag

chip brushes

hake softening brush

short-nap roller and tray

measuring tape

pencil

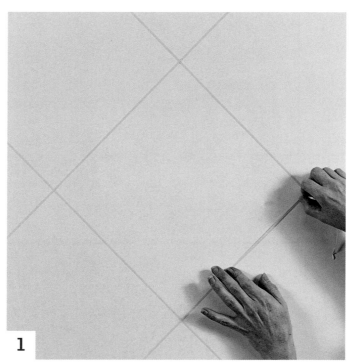

1

Measure and mark out the size of your tiles. Use a soft lead pencil or watercolor pencil to draw in the lines lightly. Don't forget to allow 1/8-inch (3mm) between the tiles for the width of your tape as you plan, measure and mark. One option is to draw a line indicating the middle of the grout line and run the tape centered on that line. Pull the tape taut enough to keep it straight but not enough to stretch it so that it becomes thinner than 1/8-inch (3mm). Burnish with your fingers or a credit card as you work.

Faux Stone Tile

2

To get a nice clean grout line with no glaze seeping underneath, roll over the taped areas with the basecoat color, Linen White. This will seal the edges of the tape. If any small amount of paint seeps under, it will be undetectable since it will be the exact same color as the basecoat.

3

Use a chip or foam brush to apply random, diagonal patches of the Berkshire Beige glaze mix to the wall. Work in an area about 2-foot (61cm) to 3-foot (91cm) square and aim for about 85% coverage, leaving some open areas. It's best to begin and end your working areas on a row of tiles.

4

Immediately apply the Fairview Taupe glaze mix in the same area, also in random, diagonal patches. Overlap and fill in areas previously untouched by the first color. Note in this picture that I have used slightly less of this color. If you wish to create a deeper, darker tile color, simply use more of this darker color. You can also vary the color usage slightly from tile to tile.

5

Take a damp terrycloth rag, fold it in half and then fold it in half again. Use it to break up and blend the colors slightly. You do not want to go for a highly blended look as was done in the "Tuscan Wall Treatment" on page 24. Leave this irregular and textural to create the illusion of stone.

6

7

Immediately take a clean, damp sea sponge and use it to "open up" random areas of the glaze, revealing the background color in textural, irregular patches. I prefer to use the back of the sponge, rather than the more prickly side, which provides more of a web-like print. It is very important when using a sponge or similar printing-type tool, to vary the position of your hand, your pressure and even the area of the sponge you are printing with. This will help to create a more organic, natural look.

Use a hake brush to soften the glaze, help to "melt" it into the background and soften the edges of the texture that you have created with the rag and the sponge. Remember, you just want to soften the finish by lightly brushing in a random direction over the surface. If you can see brushstrokes appearing in the glazed finish or are simply muddying and blending everything together you are definitely pressing too hard. Complete all of the above steps for each area before moving on.

8

9

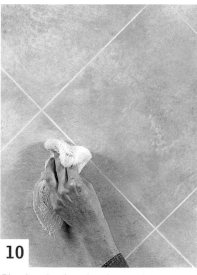

10

When the entire area has been treated to the textured finish, pull the tape. Notice that I am pulling the tape at an angle rather than straight away. This helps to break the seal of the paint/glaze.

This step softens out the finish a little while adding more depth of color. It also adds a more natural color to the grout. Simply take the Berkshire Beige paint/glaze mix and add a thin second coat over the entire area. Brush on in more open areas.

Blend and soften the glaze with a rag, and soften with the Hake brush, if necessary. This final layer should go very quickly as it is simply a toning layer.

Carved Stone Frieze

THIS ILLUSION USES A GRISAILLE technique of stenciling and hand painting to create the classic look of a carved frieze or border. Grisaille is a French term that relates to painted decoration executed in a monochromatic color scheme (shades of a single color, usually gray). It produces a lovely, soft look when done in values that are closely related. For a more dramatic look, the painting can be done with sharper contrasts in value between the highlights and shadows.

You can adapt this technique to any architectural multi-overlay stencil design. Besides creating a faux carved border, try using this technique on furniture panels, mantels or floor screens.

✏ TAKE NOTE

For this project, I have used a multi-overlay stencil that uses shadow and highlights to create the detailed illusion of a highly ornate and carved design. Creating this type of illusion requires careful attention to the relationships between the different elements. It will be necessary to shade, not only to create the look of dimension on each design element, but also to indicate how the elements overlap each other. Elements that are "on top" will receive the most amount of light and therefore will need to be highlighted in the appropriate places. Shadows need to be created on the areas where elements are blocked from the light, because they are overlapped by other elements. Practice on scrap paper first to become comfortable with a shading and highlighting scheme that will create a successful illusion.

You could simplify this technique by using a single overlay design in which you would need to shade and highlight on the individual elements, and not have to worry about shading for overlapping and to create depth.

PREPARATION

See the illustration for the measurements for laying out the stone tiles and border as shown.

Prepare the background finish as detailed in the previous technique, "Faux Stone Tile."

SUPPLIES

Royal Design Studio Stencil:

    Small Showcase Scroll

FolkArt Acrylic Colors:

    Clay Bisque

    Butter Pecan

    Medium Gray

FolkArt Extender

DecoArt Easy Blend Stencil Paint:

    Charcoal Gray

Easy Mask paper tape

³⁄₈-inch (10mm) and ⁵⁄₈-inch (16mm) stencil brushes

no. 4 filbert brush

small round brush (fitch brush)

cotton swabs

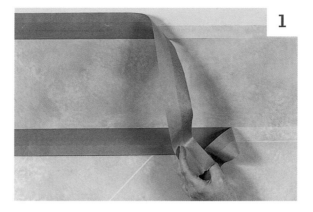

1 Use paper tape to mask off a 6¾-inch (17cm) border, 1-inch (25mm) in from the top and bottom edge of the top border area. Apply a toning layer of the Fairview Taupe paint/glaze mix, following the instructions for step 9 of the previous technique, "Faux Stone Tile." Remove the tape and allow to dry.

2 Re-tape to create two 1-inch (25mm) exposed bands at the top and bottom edges of the border area. Thin the acrylic paint colors with FolkArt Extender at a ratio of a few drops of extender per teaspoon of paint. You will be using these colors to "sculpt" form, shape and dimension out of the flat wall finish. Stencil with Clay Bisque along the top edge of the 1-inch (25mm) openings. Hug the brush to the edge, allowing just a small portion of it into the exposed area. Stencil, using an even pressure and working in small circles as you move along the edge of the tape. Alternatively, you can try sliding and scrubbing along the edge of the tape with the brush. Experiment to see which method works best for you.

3 Stencil along the lower edge in the same manner, using the Butter Pecan color. This highlight and shadow shading on the band will create the illusion that it is actually a rounded surface, protruding from the wall. The light coming from above would naturally highlight the top edge (Clay Bisque), and where it rounds away from the light at the bottom (Butter Pecan) would have a soft "form" shadow.

4 When finished, remove the tape and now place another strip of tape over the banded area, just above the bottom line. Here you will stencil a cast shadow just below. This will create the illusion that the banded area is protruding out and casting a shadow where it is blocking the light from the wall surface below it.

Carved Stone Frieze

5

The Small Showcase Scroll stencil used here is a three-overlay stencil. The first step to completing the border is to stencil all three overlays with a thin layer of Clay Bisque that has been thinned with FolkArt Extender. The idea here is not to shade, but simply to block the design in with an even value of color throughout. Use a light, even pressure to fill each design element in with translucent color.

6

This is how your border should look when you have completed all three overlays.

7

Now go back and replace each overlay one at a time. Use the Butter Pecan and a small ⅜-inch (10mm) brush to stencil along the bottom edges of each design element, just as you did with the carved border in step 3. The idea is to create a sculptural look with soft shading on the surface where it curves away from the light.

8

Use the Clay Bisque to highlight each element along the top edge, where it would naturally receive the most amount of light. Try to keep the stencil brush really tight to the edge and make your highlight very sharp there.

9 Now use the Medium Gray to create more contrast and the effect of a cast shadow on the areas where the elements overlap. Determine which elements are more "forward" and which are "behind." Apply deep shading at the point on the "behind" elements where they are overlapped by other elements which would block the light.

10 This detail shows the first overlay completed with the detailed shading and highlighting.

11 This detail shows a section that has been completed with all three overlays.

Carved Stone Frieze

12 Thin some Medium Gray with extender at a ratio of 1:1. Use a small fitch brush (or your favorite small pointed round brush) to create cast shadows on the wall surface just below the stenciled carving. Remember that the light source here is represented as coming from above. The cast shadows would fall just below the faux carving and would be connected to it, not as if it were floating in space away from the wall.

13 Use the same brush to paint stronger highlights with Clay Bisque, along the tops of some of the stronger elements.

14 Easy Blend Stencil Paint is actually oil-based paint in a solid form. I like to use it for creating really soft shading. Because it is oil-based, reserve a brush just for this particular paint as you will not be able to use the brush again with water-based acrylic paint. Load the brush by rubbing it lightly over the surface of the Easy Blend Charcoal Gray.

15 To soften the cast shadows and create a looser look to the finished illusion, swirl or drag the brush along the painted shadows.

16 Use your finger or a cotton swab to blend out the paint. Because it is oil-based it will stay wet and workable for quite a long time and it will be very easy to blend. You can also rub some into the surrounding background area here and there.

17

A detail of the finished illusion of a carved stone frieze.

Cutwork Embroidery

THIS IS A TRULY UNIQUE LOOK that uses stencils to create the illusion of cutwork embroidery. It produces a wonderful, romantic lacy effect on traditional cambric window shades. These are the "old-fashioned" roller shades that your grandmother had. Cambric is a wonderful material for painting. In fact, many professional decorative painters use it for painting samples and even for painting murals. The shades can be custom ordered with different types of trim and skirts and cut to any size.

You could also use the same material to create a lacy valance hung on a rod, as an alternative to the roll-up shade.

> ✐ **TAKE NOTE** *In order to create the cutwork embroidery look you will need to choose a "negative-type" stencil design. This is a design in which the areas that are stenciled are actually the negative spaces around the design. Take care not to choose a design with elements that are too small, which will be difficult to cut. Elements that are too large will weaken the shade.*
>
> *Depending on the stencil pattern you choose, this can be a time-consuming technique. Plan to change your blades as soon as they become dull. You may use 2–3 blades per shade, but it is worth it when cutting the small details of the design.*

THIS PRETTY PATTERN IS STENCILED right along the edge of the flap that holds the wooden slat. I ordered the shade with the decorative skirt hanging below. You can choose from many different shapes.

PREPARATION

Lay the rolled up shade flat on a large work area, such as a table. You will need a piece of glass on which to cut. Ask at your local glass supplier for a scrap piece of ¼-inch (6mm) tempered glass, which is usually cheaper. Also ask them to sand the edges to round them and make it a safe work surface. You can get a smaller piece, about 12-inches (31cm) by 18-inches (46cm), and move it along as you work.

1 Make a pencil mark at the center of the shade. Line the center of one of the design repeats on this so that the pattern ends the same at each edge. Stencil the European Lace Border design in Burnt Umber. Most of this will be cut away, so all that will be left is a thin line of color outlining the "cutwork", as if it were embroidered. Stencil with an even, solid color.

2 Because I did not want to cut the pattern to the edge, I measured off ½-inch (13mm) and placed a piece of tape there so that it would remain unpainted.

Cutwork Embroidery

3 Place the shade on glass and cut out shapes with the swivel knife. The blade turns 360 degrees, meaning that both you and the object that you are cutting can remain stationary. Try to cut just inside the outer edge of the stenciling, leaving approximately 1/16-inch (1.5mm) to 1/8-inch (3mm) of color.

4 Cut the smaller elements first. Try to keep the knife in constant contact with the surface during the course of cutting each shape, rather than removing and replacing it. When you come to corners and points in the design, simply rotate the knife blade and continue cutting. This detail shows the finished cutting. You can see that there are some imperfections and unevenness when you look closely. This is inevitable and will not be noticeable when the shade is hanging. Trust me!

Lace-Edge Shade Skirt

ORDER A SHADE WITH THE DESIRED AMOUNT OF CAMBRIC HANGING BELOW TO ACCOMMODATE THE DEPTH of your design, plus several inches. I special ordered this shade to have a plain skirt hanging below the wooden rod, which was 8-inches (203mm) deep. This romantic shade was stenciled with a floral embroidery panel design. The Lace-Edge Skirt uses the same supplies and preparation as the European Lace Shade.

Position the design as desired and stencil. I wanted to use just the lower portion of this Persian Lace design, so the stencil was pushed up.

The flap covers the upper part of the stencil, so I merely taped it to hold it up. Then I stenciled almost to the top edge.

Lace-Edge Shade Skirt

Cut the cambric with the swivel knife. For this pattern, just cut out the large elements. The other elements are entirely too small to cut effectively.

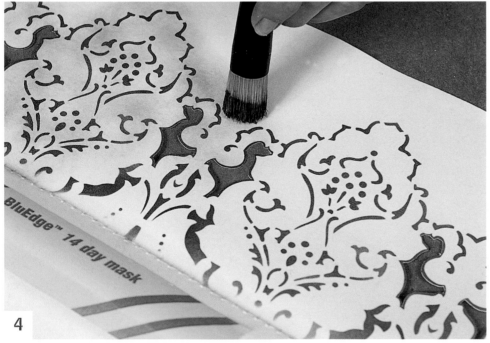

Use a large stencil brush to swirl a light blush of the Burnt Umber color over the lace area. Use a very dry brush along with a light pressure. This will provide a nice antique, tea-stained look. Just allow the color to fade out below the design. This will be cut away later anyway.

5 Follow in the same manner with the Potpourri Rose, just lightly brushing the color into the background.

6
Use the swivel knife to carefully cut along the lacy edge of the border, as defined by the stencil design.

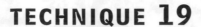

TECHNIQUE 19

Faux Panel Moldings

THE PLAIN WALLS of this formerly boring bedroom were transformed into an enchanting, formal backdrop for the French-inspired colors and furnishings. Real carved moldings are costly and require a skilled carpenter to install them correctly. You can create instant architecture without ever touching a saw or a hammer! With a simple, single overlay molding stencil and a few tricks with tape and stencil shading you can create the elegant and expensive look of fine, carved moldings.

This illusion can also be used to create a carved look or panels on hollow core doors, furniture, walls and even real crown molding. All that is required is keen attention to detail for measuring and taping, and shading with a simple stencil brush.

TAKE NOTE *While this technique is shown on plain white panels, you could also have fun trying this on faux wood or marble or on plain mirror frames. The panels could be placed around a treasured piece of art, from floor to ceiling, above a chair rail as shown or just below a painted chair rail with an allover pattern stenciled above. The choices are all yours.*

PREPARATION

Base coat the wall with two coats of Linen White. Allow to dry a minimum of two days. Plan out your panel placement by drawing out sketches of the walls to scale on graph paper. The size and shape of the panels are up to you. These panels were done above a painted chair rail and dado treatment. They were centered vertically between the ceiling line and the line of the stenciled chair rail. The width of the panels varies on each wall, but I tried to space them equally apart (8 inches (20cm), in this case) and kept them the same, uniform distance from the floor and ceiling. The pencil lines were drawn using a large bubble level to get them level and plum and to indicate the outside edge of the panels. The tape is run just inside the pencil lines. Once you have the tape in place, you will have a good visual of how size and scale work in the project area. Any necessary adjustments can be easily made prior to painting.

    Mix two separate glazes using the Richmond Gold and Valley Forge Brown with AquaGlaze at a ratio of 1:4. The paints may look more brown than gold. Once you mix them with the glaze and make them more translucent, the color will appear much more gold than before.

1 Seal the edges of the tape with the wall base color. This will prevent any of the glaze from seeping under the edges of the tape. You can use a stencil brush (as shown) or simply use a short nap roller and paint right over the tape.

2 Using the technique outlined in chapter 2, technique 1, for creating the first layer of the Tuscan Wall Treatment, apply the Richmond Gold glaze mix to the entire wall area (one small, workable area at a time.) Use a 3-inch (76mm) foam brush or a small roller to apply irregular diagonal patches of glaze to the wall.

Faux Panel Moldings

3

Immediately use the Ultimate Stippler to blend out and soften the glaze, creating a thin, uneven "blush" of color. Let dry.

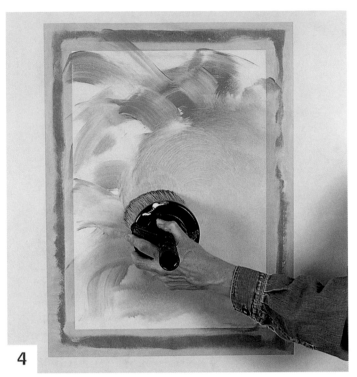

4

Create a darker value in just the centers of the panels by going back over them with the Valley Forge Brown glaze mixture.

5

Soften out any brushstrokes with a hake brush. Use the brush to lightly skim over just the surface of the wet glaze, smoothing out any indication of brush marks. Let dry.

6

Remove the tape, exposing a band of 2-inch (51mm) wide Linen White that will now become your "molding".

7

Use a grid ruler to mark a light pencil line from each inside corner to outside corner. This is your miter line. Real molding is always cut at an angle at the corners to make a frame.

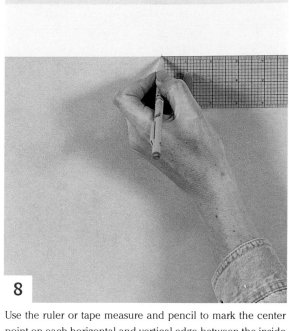

8

Use the ruler or tape measure and pencil to mark the center point on each horizontal and vertical edge, between the inside corners. You will center one repeat of the design on this line, which ensures that the pattern will end at the same place at each of the mitered edges.

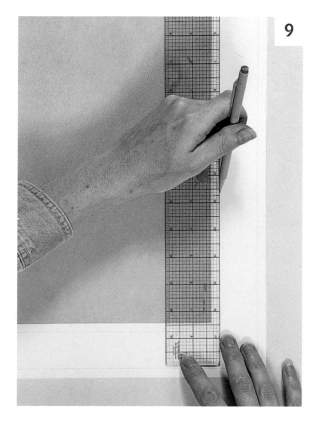

9

Use your grid ruler to mark a light pencil line ⅜-inch (10mm) in from the inside edge of all the moldings. This is where you will line up the inside edge of the stencil design (not the stencil itself). If you choose to use a different molding design than the one shown, you may need to adjust the width of your molding and determine where you will make your mark to center the design between the edges.

Faux Panel Moldings

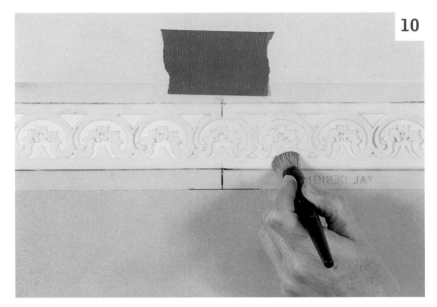

10 Center your design on the center marks that you made and begin stenciling from there to each edge. The whole design will first be stenciled solidly and lightly with Barnwood. Thin the acrylic paint with extender at a rate of a few drops per teaspoon of paint to make it flow better.

11 At the corners of the molding line you are working on, place tape just outside the miter line that you drew in, so that the design will end abruptly there.

12 When you work on the adjoining line of molding, simply switch the tape placement to the opposite side of the line.

13 Once all of the stenciling has been completed with the acrylic color, Barnwood, you will go back and add more detailed shading and contrast with the Easy Blend paint. Easy Blend is an oil-based paint in a solid form that is ideal for soft shading. Because it stays wet and moveable, it is easy to create a very smooth effect. See pages 104–105 (Carved Stone Frieze) for more detail on using Easy Blend paint. At this point, you will be using the same shading technique that is detailed in the "Decorative Carved Dado" technique on pages 83–85. Here the negative stencil has much smaller open areas.

14

The stenciling now will be much more limited and concentrated only in the areas that would receive the least amount of light. Here, the light source is represented as coming from the upper right, so the shading is confined to the upper right sides of all the open areas. If these were actually carved into the surface, the light would not be hitting these areas at all and they would be in the deepest shadow. Because the relationship of the molding to the light changes as you move around the panel, different areas of the design details will receive the deepest shading on the top, bottom, left and right sides.

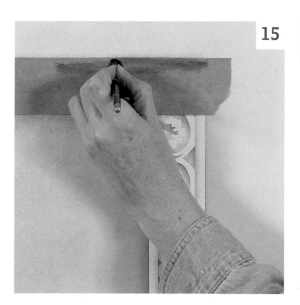

15 Once you've completed the carved detailing, it's time to define the shape of the molding piece itself. Use paper tape to mask off the straight edges and shade right along the edge of the tape.

Faux Panel Moldings

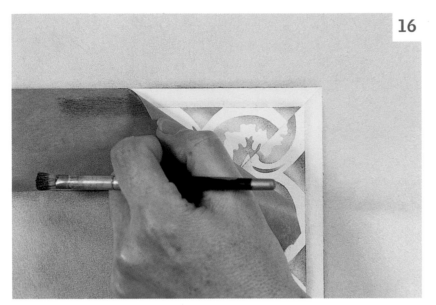

16 Here I have shaded along the top right edge where the molding meets the wall. In reality this area would not have a shadow, just a slight change in value. In order to visually separate the molding from the wall for this illusion, I have shaded it just slightly to create a subtle contrast between the two surface planes. Next, move the tape down ⅜-inch (10mm) and stencil just above the tape again to define the change in the shape of the molding there.

17 At the bottom of that molding piece, create the deepest shading where the molding meets the wall. The protruding molding would cast a much deeper shadow here. Then move the tape up (shown) to the next line and create a shadow along that line as well.

18 To create the illusion that the molding rounds out away from the wall and towards the viewer, move the tape to the other side of the line and create a soft-form shadow. This is different from a cast shadow. It is the effect of light (or lack of it) on the actual surface of the object. These shadows are lighter, but definitely provide the illusion of roundness.

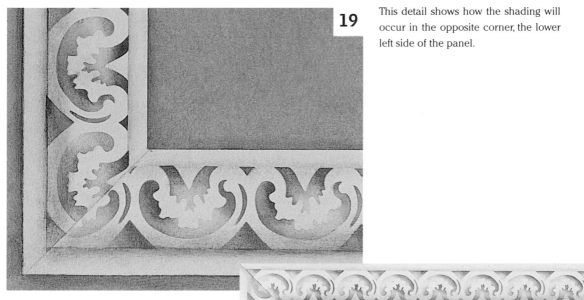

19 This detail shows how the shading will occur in the opposite corner, the lower left side of the panel.

A detail of the finished panel.

More Ideas & Inspiration

GOLD FRAMED PRINT

*Gallery-wrapped canvas becomes an elegant piece of faux-framed art. The delicately stenciled flower vase is enhanced by a frame of rich gold, using the same shading techniques outlined in **"Faux Panel Moldings."***

FAUX CARVED FIREPLACE MANTEL

*This simple wood mantelpiece was treated to some intricate "carving" with some fairly simple stencil shading. This technique, outlined in **"Decorative Carved Dado"** can also be used on crown moldings, doors and anywhere you want to add a special detail to plain wood.*

MARQUETRY WALL SHELF

*A plain plank of oak gets a "Royal" treatment with the addition of some decorative molding and a **"Faux Marquetry"** treatment that is easily achieved with a simple stencil and wood stain.*

FOLK EMBROIDERED WALL FINISH

*A folk flower border gets some extra flourish with embossing and over-painting to create the look of **"Crewel Embroidery."** Bold colors add extra punch.*

More Ideas, continued

ADD A LITTLE FLOURISH

*This bathroom wall treatment uses the same stenciling technique featured in **"Oriental Brocade,"** but with a twist. Here, a warm, lighter shadow color is used and the whole wall is treated to a stria over-glaze to further soften the look. The plain cabinet doors become embossed metal with raised stenciling and a metallic paint finish.*

WISTERIA WALL

*Free-form wisteria vines frame an antique iron bed in this romantic room setting. Individual clusters of
leaves and flowers are stenciled from a simple hand-painted vine for a completely custom application.*

More Ideas, continued

TOILE FOR THE WALL

Here, the same designs used for the **"Cutwork Embroidery"** shade are stenciled in a bold panel treatment to create a great focal point and setting for the blue transferware plates.

TOILE DETAIL

The detail photo shows how the rich, clear blue color and accented stencil shading technique combine to recreate the classic look of a monochromatic Toile du Jouy fabric.

COURTYARD WALL WITH STONE FRIEZE

A courtyard wall is recreated with architectural stencil designs coupled with well-defined shading and attention to detail. Find out how to create a similar look in this book under **"Carved Stone Frieze"** and **"Faux Panel Moldings"**.

OLD LINEN WALL TREATMENT

*Here is another take on the **"Printed Linen"** wall finish shown in this book. Here, the textured finish was treated to a coat of warm silver paint that was over-glazed to add depth, tone and "age".*

CASBAH WALL TREATMENT

This finish was designed to copy the look of an expensive wallpaper treatment. Three different stencil patterns combine with translucent glazes in Ochres and Siennas to create a look that wraps the room with a warm ambience.

Resources

STENCILS & RELATED PRODUCTS

ROYAL DESIGN STUDIO

2504 Transportation Ave., Suite H

National City, CA 91950

www.royaldesignstudio.com

800-747-9767

All of the stencil designs as well as most of the tools, products, paints, glazes and texture mediums used throughout this book are available through the Royal Design Studio catalog and website.

MODELLO DESIGNS

2504 Transportation Ave, Suite H

National City, CA 91950

www.modellodesigns.com

800-663-3860

Custom decorative masking patterns for glass, wood, concrete, paint and plaster. Custom-sized and cut to order.

PAINTS & RELATED PRODUCTS

FAUX EFFECTS, INTERNATIONAL/INC.

3535 Aviation Blvd.

Vero Beach, FL 32960

www.fauxfx.com

800-270-8871

Manufacturer of Aqua Finishing Solutions and Gold Label Architectural Coatings, including AquaBond, AquaSeal, AquaColor, AquaGlaze, Stain & Seal, Dutch Metal Paints and LusterStone.

MODERN MASTERS, INC.

13201 Saticoy St.

North Hollywood, CA 91605

www.modernmastersinc.com

800-942-3166

Manufacturer of a full line of metallic paints and decorative finishing mediums.

MISCELLANEOUS

SCUMBLE GOOSIE

www.sgoosie.com

866-801-0017

Unpainted furniture and decorative accessories

BLINDS CONNECTION

www.blindsconnection.com

888-397-3768

Source for custom cambric shades in many styles and colors

HOME/HARDWARE CENTERS

These big chain stores are one-stop shopping for paints, texturing products, brushes, rollers, drop cloths, drywall mix, glue and other assorted painting accessories.

FOR MORE INSPIRATION AND INFORMATION:

THE STENCIL ARTISANS LEAGUE, INC.

www.sali.org

A non-profit educational organization committed to promoting stenciling and the related decorative arts through area and online chapters and an annual convention and stencil and faux finish exposition.

MURALSPLUS

www.muralsplus.com

An online community project for all muralists, stencilers and faux and decorative painters. Features an active and informative community message board, an extensive photo gallery of members work and a decorative painter directory. Membership is free.

Index

The best in decorative painting instruction and inspiration is from North Light Books!

DECORATIVE MINI-MURALS

Add drama to any room in your home with one of these eleven delightful mini-murals! They're perfect when you don't have the time or the experience to tackle a whole wall. You'll learn exactly which colors and brushes to use. And there are tips and mini-demos on how to get that realistic "wow" effect mural painters love. Detailed templates, photos and instructions assure your success at every step.

ISBN 1-58180-145-9, paperback, 144 pages, #31891-K

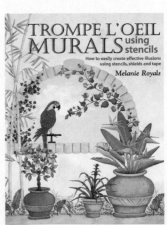

DECORATIVE ARTIST'S GUIDE TO REALISTIC PAINTING

Take your decorative painting to an exciting new level of depth and dimension by creating the illusion of reality—one that transforms your work from good to extraordinary! Patti DeRenzo, CDA, shows you how to master the building blocks of realism—value, temperature, intensity and form—to render three-dimensional images with height, depth and width.

ISBN 0-89134-995-2, paperback, 128 pages, #31661-K

These books and other fine North Light titles are available from your local art & craft retailer, bookstore, online supplier or by calling 1-800-448-0915.

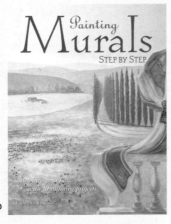

PAINTING MURALS STEP-BY-STEP

Charles Grund takes the fear out of painting large, beautiful murals that fool the eye and stir the soul. Full color, step-by-step instructions provide you with the confidence and skills you need to design and paint amazing wall murals. You'll find eleven projects with a variety of themes suitable for almost any room.

ISBN 1-58180-141-6, paperback, 144 pages, #31890-K

TROMPE L'OEIL MURALS USING STENCILS

Learn how to create stunning illusions on walls, floors, and ceilings. Here is all the instruction you need to use inexpensive, laser-cut plastic stencils with skill and confidence. Author Melanie Royals shows you how to combine stencils, shields and tape with simple paint techniques, buy the proper equipment, prepare surfaces, manipulate stencils and apply paint. The final section provides more advanced instruction for large-scale projects.

ISBN 1-58180-028-2, paperback, 128 pages, #31668-K

PAINTING GILDED FLORALS AND FRUITS

Learn how to enhance your paintings with the classic elegance of decorative gold, silver and variegated accents. Rebecca Baer illustrates detailed gilding techniques with step-by-step photos and invaluable problem-solving advice. Perfect for your home or gift giving, there are 13 exciting projects in all, each one enhanced with lustrous leafing effects.

ISBN 1-58180-261-7, paperback, 144 pages, #32126-K